THE WHOLE TRUTH

About the

Catholic Church

and the

HOLY BIBLE

And Frequently Asked Questions

FR. JOHN NOONE

Jesus said, *I Am the Way and the Truth and the Life.* (John 14:6)

You shall know the Truth, and the Truth will set you free. (John 8:32)

The Spirit will guide you to all Truth. (John 16:13)

Formatted for eBook and POD book by Booknook.biz.

Fr. John Noone's Books can be found on
https://frjohnnoonesbooks.wordpress.com/

ISBN 978-1-7351946-2-2

Table of Contents

Introduction

Christ is the Center of History. God became a man. History is the story of God interacting with His people. History is His Story.

> *To be ignorant of what occurred before you were born is always to remain a child.*
>
> (Cicero 106-43 B.C. Roman Author)

> *Those who do not know history's mistakes are doomed to repeat them.*
>
> (Sir Edmund Burke 1729-1797)

As Catholics our faith is rooted in actual historical facts.

The story of the Catholic Church is an extraordinary story – it is the story of Jesus Christ imparting the Truth to the Church He founded, and the efforts of that Church to protect and proclaim that Truth so that people can get to know it and get to heaven. It is a story of saints and scholars, of heroes and heretics, of prophets, politicians and popes, of courage, corruption and power struggles, of persecution and prejudice, of martyrs and missionaries, of good and evil.

The Catholic Church should not be in existence today. It has faced enemies for without and within. For the past 2,000 years it has been betrayed by bishops, priests, religious and lay people. It has been attacked by emperors, kings, queens and politicians. But, on account of its Divine Founder, Jesus Christ and the Holy Spirit, the Spirit of Truth, it has survived the many attempts to undermine and defeat it. And it will continue. Jesus said that He would be with His Church until the end of time, and the gates of hell would not prevail against it.

This booklet points out some of the most important events in the 2000-year history of the Catholic Church and the Bible, and hopefully, it will instill a desire to learn more of the Full Truth of the Catholic Church and the Bible.

Part One – History of the Catholic Church

The apostles cast lots and added Matthias to their number, in place of Judas, as the twelfth apostle. The authority for this action is to be found in a prophetic psalm of David. After receiving the power of the Holy Spirit which had been promised to them, so that they could work miracles and proclaim the truth, they first bore witness to their faith in Jesus Christ and established churches throughout Judea.

They then went out into the whole world and proclaimed to the nations the same doctrinal faith.

(Tertullian, priest, theologian and apologist c. 160-c. 220)
(Acts 1:16-20; Ps 69:25; Ps 109:8)

The Apostles proclaimed the truth which Jesus that taught them.

1st Century

Jesus died about 33 A.D. The Holy Spirit came upon His disciples (followers) at Pentecost. This changed the group, which was filled with fear, into a group filled with wisdom and courage and all the gifts of the Holy Spirit. They began to preach in Jerusalem and many people were converted to be followers of Christ. But some people rose up against them, and Stephen, a deacon, was stoned to death. Saul, who was a leader of those who opposed the followers of Christ, had a conversion experience while on the road to Damascus. He, from then on, was an outstanding follower of Christ and came to be known as Paul, the Apostle to the Gentiles. He traveled a great deal in order to preach about Christ and wrote many letters to instruct and to meet the needs of the followers of Christ. We have several of those letters in the New Testament.

The first disciples were Jewish. Some of the Gentiles also became disciples. Then the question arose as to whether the Gentiles had to follow the Jewish law. Some said "yes". Some said "no", and Paul was one of those who said "no". A Council was held in Jerusalem about 50 A.D. Peter presided over that Council. The decision was made that the Gentiles were not bound by Jewish law.

About 42 A.D., persecution of the disciples of Christ arose. James the Greater, an Apostle, was martyred (killed for the faith) and the disciples fled to different cities – Rome, Alexandria, and Antioch. It was at Antioch that the disciples were called "Christian" for the first time (Acts 11:26).

There was a fire in Rome which destroyed much of the city. Nero, the emperor, blamed the Christians and began to persecute them. Peter and Paul were martyred in this persecution which lasted only a year (c. 65 A.D.), but it instilled an attitude of hostility towards the Christians that lasted for about 300 years. This hostility burst forth at different times in different places in the Roman Empire and thousands of Christians were martyred.

The Romans destroyed Jerusalem in 70 A.D. Before this time Mark wrote his Gospel.

Matthew and Luke wrote their Gospels before 80 A.D. John wrote his Gospel around 100 A.D. These four Gospels tell us about what Jesus said and did.

At first, the disciples thought that Jesus would return soon, but as time went on, they realized that this was not the case. Jesus did not tell his followers:

1. to write a sacred book,
2. to define doctrines; that is, the body of revealed and defined Truth which His followers were bound to hold.
3. how to structure His Church,
4. how to worship,
5. or even how to sum up what they believed (a creed).

So, they began to do those things in order to preserve the truth which Jesus had taught.

> But, when He comes, the Spirit of Truth, He will guide you to all truth. Jn 16:13

2nd Century

Christians were scattered around the Roman Empire – Syria, Greece, Turkey and Egypt in the East. In the West also there were Christians in Italy, Gaul (France) and North Africa. John the Apostle died around 100 A.D. The followers of Christ were first called "The Catholic Church" by Ignatius of Antioch in 107 A.D. as he was being brought as a prisoner to Rome to be thrown to the lions.

The Catholic Church became more organized – bishops, priests and deacons were appointed.

Some Romans felt threatened by the Church and persecutions occurred at different times and places.

A big problem faced by the Church was the emergence of heresies or false teachings.

So, the question was:

What Is The Truth?

Some, known as Gnostics, said that their teachings had been passed along secretly in Gnostic groups from the time of the Apostles. Marcion, a bishop, said that all the Old Testament should be rejected. Montanus emphasized religious extremes and the imminent second coming of Christ. Irenaeus, a Gallic theologian, said that all Christian teaching came from the Apostles and that their teaching is to be found in Scripture and Tradition - the Scriptures being the Old Testament, certain early Apostolic writings and also Tradition which was the public teachings of the bishops of dioceses founded by the Apostles.

The big question continued:

What Is The Truth?

A document called the Didache was written at this time. It tells what the Catholic Christians of this time believed, how they practiced this faith, and how the Church was organized.

> The Spirit is the one that testifies, and the Spirit is Truth.
> 1 Jn 5:6

3rd Century

During this century there was a great deal of thought put into the teachings of the Catholic Church. In North Africa, Tertullian (c. 160-220) and Cyprian (d. 258) wrote theological works and, for the first time, used words like "Trinity" and "Sacrament." In Alexandria, Egypt, theologians like Clement (d. 215) and Origen (c.185-254) brought Greek philosophy into their theology. This approach would be standard for scholastic theologians in the Middle Ages (500-1500).

Pope Callistus I (c. 217-222) said that Christians could receive penance when they needed remission from their sins. From 249-251 the Catholic Church was persecuted under the Emperor Decius. Those who denied the faith were called "Lapsi." When the persecution was over many of the "Lapsi" wanted to return to the Church after doing penance. Some said they could not, but the Roman Church said they could return.

In 256, Pope Stephen I said that Baptism, which was administered by heretics, was valid.

Christian art made its first appearance in the Catacombs in Rome. Also, Christians began to make statues.

Persecution of the Church continued. Around 292 A.D., the Emperor Diocletian divided the Roman Empire into the East and West. Rome was the chief city in the West, and Constantinople in the East. Rome began to lose its influence from this time on.

4th Century

This is a most important time in the history of the Catholic Church. Constantine I (306-337), the Emperor, converted to Christianity. This ended the persecutions, and Christians could evangelize freely. The Emperors and wealthy people built magnificent churches, especially in Constantinople and Rome.

A priest from Alexandria, Egypt, named Arius denied that Christ was God. This was the worst heresy, or false teaching, of the early Church because it was so popular that it had its own bishops, priests and churches.

Then the question had to be:

What Is The Truth?

The Council of Nicaea in 325 affirmed the equality and divinity of the Father and the Son. However, the Arian heresy continued. In 381, the Council of Constantinople I reaffirmed the teaching of Nicaea and taught the equality and divinity of the Holy Spirit also. The Council gave us the Nicene Creed which is said at Mass every Sunday in the Catholic Church. Orthodox and the vast majority of the Protestant denominations accept this creed or set of beliefs. Greco-Roman philosophical terms began to be used, like "persons" of the Trinity sharing in one divine "substance."

Antony (251-356) set up a foundation for hermits in the desert in Egypt near the Red Sea. They wanted to devote themselves totally to solitude, prayer and fasting.

God raised up intellectual giants at this time. Athanasius (296-373) bishop of Alexandria, Egypt, Ambrose (340-397), bishop of Milan, John Chrysostom (c. 347-407) bishop of Constantinople, Augustine of Hippo (354-430) and Jerome (342-420) who was a biblical scholar and translated the Bible into Latin, the language of the common people – hence the translation is called the *Vulgate.*

At the Council of Rome in 382, the official list of the inspired books of the Bible was accepted. Toward the end of the century the barbarians began to invade the Roman Empire in the West.

> But when He comes, the Spirit of Truth, He will guide you to all truth. Jn 16:13

5th Century

Barbarians, people who were not Greek or Roman (Germanic, Celts, Slavs), poured into the Roman Empire in the West and took over. There was now no government structure and cities fell into ruin. Rome itself was captured in 410. The Roman Empire came to an end in Western Europe in 476. Then began what we call the Middle Ages.

There were some bright spots. Augustine of Hippo (354-430), North Africa, a strong defender of orthodox or true doctrine composed his theological works. These works have influenced thought for centuries, even up to today. The popes strengthened their authority. Pope Leo the Great (440-461) convinced Attila, the Hun, not to destroy Rome in 452. The Council of Ephesus in 431 declared that Mary is the Mother of God. At the Council of Chalcedon in 451 a letter from Pope Leo was read. It said that Christ is one person with two natures, one human, one divine, each distinct but both united in one person. The attending Bishops accepted this teaching with enthusiasm. It is the teaching of the Catholic Church since then and is accepted by Orthodox and the vast majority of Protestant denominations.

Patrick arrived in Ireland in 432, and by the time of his death in c. 461 nearly all of the country had become Catholic.

When the Roman Empire fell in the year 410 in Western Europe, it marked the end of ancient history. The next thousand years, c.500 A.D. to c.1500 A.D. is known as the Medieval Period or the Middle Ages.

Rome was a devastated city by the end of the 5th century.

6th Century

During this century the Catholic Church saw the beginning of its separation into the East and the West. The Western section of the Roman Empire was now under the control of the barbarians or those who were not of the Greek or Roman culture. The Eastern section was ruled by the Byzantine Emperor in Constantinople. He still considered the West to be under his authority. The Emperor, Justinian I (527-565), took back Italy and wanted the popes to do his bidding. The popes tried to remain independent. In 568, the Lombard barbarians conquered some major cities of the Byzantines resulting in the West being ruled by barbarians and not Byzantines.

The barbarian invasions brought about a great deal of chaos. Much would have been lost had it not been for the monasteries and popes.

The popes helped to keep the Church alive. Gregory the Great (590-604) concentrated on the West and the evangelization of the barbarians. He sent Augustine, a Benedictine monk, to Canterbury in England in 597 to convert the pagan Anglo-Saxons. Augustine of Canterbury is called "the Apostle to the English Church".

Men and women wanted to pray and fast in the company of others. This gave rise to Monasticism. A Monastery was a dwelling place for people, usually men, who wanted to be alone and pray. These men were called monks. The word monk comes from the Greek word monos, which means alone. They took 3 vows: (1) Poverty – they own nothing; (2) Chastity – never to marry and to live pure lives; (3) Obedience – obey the abbot or superior.

These monks prayed and worked. They worked the land, taught people how to farm and raise cattle, sheep and vegetables. They copied ancient manuscripts on sheepskin or calfskin (vellum) thus ensuring that these works would not be lost. They copied the Bible and classics (relating to the ancient Greek and Roman world). In monasteries there were rooms (scriptoria) where the monks copied these manuscripts. Many of these books were decorated (illuminated) in beautiful colors and designs. The monks were historians (chroniclers) because they recorded events of the time in which they lived. These writings are called *Chronicles.* The monks preserved the Catholic Christian truth and culture and gradually transformed the pagan culture around them.

In many of the monasteries there were large churches, living quarters for the monks, infirmaries, and housing for guests and laborers. These monasteries kept the faith alive during the 5th though the 10th centuries. They gradually changed the pagan culture around them. Knowledge of theology, science and secular topics, preserved by the monks, formed the foundation for the universities which were to come in the 11th and 12th centuries. The faith passed on by the monks influenced the development of law and culture and the ideas of the rights of man.

In ancient Greece and Rome, there was no University System as we have it today with its faculties, courses, examinations, graduate and undergraduate studies and degrees. This system of education came into being in the Medieval Period when the Catholic Church was the only institution in Europe to show consistent interest in the cultivation of knowledge. The popes were the greatest protectors of the Universities.

The Catholic Church also introduced something else which was not in ancient Greece or Rome, and that was works of charity. Thousands of young Catholic women entered religious life to devote themselves to God, to hospital work and to the service of the sick.

The barbarians gradually became civilized. Missionaries such as Patrick, Boniface, Cyril and Methodius, Augustine of Canterbury, Adelbert and Ansgar worked to bring the truth of God's Word to the barbarians. Catholic Christianity was always closely connected with Graeco-Roman civilization, so automatically the missionaries shared the Gospel along with this civilization. The culture of Europe would be a combination of Grecian, Roman, Catholic Christianity and Barbarian.

Monasticism was the chief instrument which served to civilize the barbarians. There were different types – Basilian, Benedictine and Celtic. The Benedictine proved to be the popular one in Europe. It was moderate, flexible and detailed. The Rule provided guidelines for all sorts of men. These monasteries were centers of sanctification, conversion and learning.

The monks in monasteries worked to: (1) Convert the barbarians and (2) Civilize them.

Founders and promoters of monasteries were:

Benedict c. 480-550 (Italy) who is the Patron Saint of Europe;
Cassiodorus c. 485-580 (Italy);
Columba 521-597 (Ireland) who is a Patron Saint of Ireland & Scotland;
Columbanus c. 540-615 (Ireland).

Cassiodorus established a monastery at Vivarium, Italy. He emphasized the scholarly life, and there was a wealth of scholarly works in the monastery. Columba left Ireland (c.590) and brought Celtic monasteries to eastern Gaul (modern-day France) and northern Italy. St. Benedict set up a monastery in Monte Cassino, Italy, which is acknowledged as one of the first and most influential of the monasteries.

7th Century

In this century, the big change was brought about by Mohammed who said that he had visions which he believed were from Allah, the only true God. He united and converted the Arabs in the Arabian Peninsula.

He died in 632. His followers began to take over the Holy Land, North Africa and Egypt – places that were strongly Catholic for centuries. Some scholars, who fled from Islam, came to Rome and had a strong influence there. In a period of about 100 years (c. 642-752) there were several Greek-speaking popes. All of these popes insisted on the primacy of the pope and his independence from the Emperor.

Ireland, at this time, was almost completely Catholic. The process of the conversion of the Anglo-Saxon in England was proceeding well. France, too, was converting.

8th Century

In 711, the Muslims conquered Spain and then marched into France. However, they were defeated at Poitiers by Charles Martel. This victory saved Western Christendom.

Boniface, the Apostle of Germany, spread the Gospel there. He strongly supported the pope. The grandson of Charles Martel, Charlemagne, or Charles the Great (768-814), worked closely with the pope and helped the pope to defend papal lands against attacks by the Lombards. Charlemagne did a great deal to reform the Church through Liturgy (the official prayer of the Church) and education. He chose Alcuin, an Englishman, to organize a palace school, which became a center of intellectual leadership.

Charlemagne wanted to rule the Church, but the popes resisted. On December 25, 800 A.D., Charlemagne was crowned Roman Emperor by Pope Leo III. By doing this the pope was reviving the Western side of the Roman Empire which had been dead since the 5th century.

In England, the Venerable Bede wrote the first history of the English people. In Ireland, monks produced many works of art including the Book of Kells, which is preserved in the Library of Trinity College, Dublin. It dates to about 800 A.D.

A movement began, called Iconoclasm, which held that the use of images, like statues or paintings, was idolatry. This movement was started in the East by the Emperor Leo III in 726 and caused confusion in the East until 842. The Iconoclasts (meaning "breakers of images") used the biblical ban on graven images as their argument against icons.

So, the question was, "could statues and icons be used"?

What Is The Truth?

The Council of Nicaea II in 787 condemned this movement. So, statues and icons could be used to remind people of Jesus, Mary, the saints, etc.

9th Century

In 814, Charlemagne died. His empire was divided, but it quickly fell apart. However, his emphasis on education continued and scholars from Spain, Ireland, Italy and England went to the French court. These scholars created handwriting and manuscripts of Gregorian chant.

New pagans arrived on the scene. They were from Scandinavia and were known as Vikings. They attacked monasteries in Iona, Scotland, and Ireland. Learning went on a downward trend throughout the Western Church. The Frankish state fell. This was followed by a struggle for power. Noble families in Rome tried to control the Pope, but he fought for independence.

From 858 to 867 and from 877 to 886, Photius was Patriarch of Constantinople. The Photian schism began. It brought confusion in relations between the East and the West. In 865, Ansgar, apostle of Scandinavia, died. In 869-885, Cyril and Methodius (brothers), the apostles of the Slavs, devised an alphabet and translated the Gospels and liturgy into the Slavonic language.

10th Century

The 10th century was filled with trouble. Attacks on Europe came from all sides – Vikings from Scandinavia, Muslims from Spain and North Africa and the Magyars from Asia. The noble families in Rome tried to control the papacy as a way to rule Rome. In the early 900's, three popes were murdered. John XII was only 18 years old when his family acquired the papacy for him.

God, however, always raises up great saints in time of need. Dunstan (909-988) in England worked hard to reform the Church there. But the most important reform movement was started by the duke of Aquitaine (France), William the Pious. In 910, he founded the monastery of Cluny in south-central France, and over 1,000 other monasteries sprang from it.

The German King, Otto I (936-973), was crowned Emperor by Pope John XII and in this way established the Holy Roman Empire which would last until the 19th century. Like many others, Otto wanted to control the pope, but on account of the distance between Germany and Rome and the political confusion of the time, he was unable to fulfill his wishes.

11th Century

In this century the struggle between the popes and the Holy Roman emperors continued. The emperors chose popes, but the popes tried to achieve independence from the emperors. Pope Nicholas II (1059-1061) decreed that the Roman Cardinals would elect the pope in the future. This was done in 1061, when they elected Pope Alexander II.

The year 1054 is a sad year in the history of the Catholic Church. The Eastern Schism occurred. A schism is a conscious and willful separation of a group from the unity of the Church and the authority of the Pope. The Pope's representative, Humbert, and Michael Cerularius, Patriarch of Constantinople, excommunicated each other. This brought to a head the growing separation between the Church in the East and the Church in the West. It had begun when Constantine, in the 4th century, moved his capitol from Rome to a new city, Constantinople, which he called after himself. The split involved not just theology, but also politics, culture, personalities and lust for power. This separated the Orthodox (or Eastern Churches) from unity with the Pope and the Western Church. Since 1965, heroic efforts have been made by Pope Paul VI, Patriarch Athenagoras of Constantinople, Pope John Paul II and Pope Benedict XVI to heal the division. Pope John Paul II said that the Church should breathe with two lungs – East and West.

In 1073, Pope Gregory VII was determined to make the papacy free from lay control. Lay Investiture was a problem at that time. This was a ceremony in which the lay lord gave a bishop the tokens of office (crozier, ring, vestments, hence the word investiture). Gregory said that this could only be done by the Pope. The German emperor, Henry IV, disagreed. Gregory excommunicated him. Henry begged for forgiveness and received it, but strengthened his control on the German Church. All kings, at this time, considered that they had control over the Church in their own kingdom.

Pope Gregory VII firmly established Rome as the undisputed spiritual leader of the Church in the West.

Pope Urban II (1088-1099) set the crusades into motion in 1095. The name "Crusade" comes from the cross which was embroidered on the garments worn by those taking part in the Crusades. The Crusades were military expeditions first called by Pope Urban II and undertaken by Western Europe in order to retake the Holy Land from the Muslims who had originally taken it from the Catholics. Those Crusades – 8 in all – lasted almost 200 years from 1096-1270. There were many factors involved. Deep piety and heroic sacrifices on the part of many people were evident. Other people got involved in the crusades for political, economic, or selfish motives, and also for the adventure. They involved hundreds of thousands of people from every country and background. The 4th Crusade of 1204, against the directives of the Pope, attacked the city of Constantinople which resulted in a lot of death and destruction. This caused great bitterness between the Greek Orthodox and Catholic Church. It lasts even to today. The 5th Crusade (1217-1221) is called "The Children's Crusade." It is estimated that about 40,000 children, mostly from Germany and France, went to help, but ended up in Muslim slave markets. The Crusades failed to restore Palestine as a Christian Kingdom. The Crusades opened up trade and travel between Europe and the Middle East. But there were negative results also – the gap between the Church in the East and the Church in the West was widened and a great deal of scandal was caused by these expeditions.

12th Century

The Renaissance began in this period. It stretched from approximately the 1200's to the 1500's. The Renaissance was a time of rebirth or flowering in cultural and intellectual pursuits. It brought profound advances in economic, political and scientific life. Religious life was also changed and its effects are felt in the Church up to today. This period is one of the most important periods in the history of the West and a bridge between the Middle Ages (about 500 to about 1500) and the modern world. There was a strong economy, and consequently, large Churches could be built. On account of flying buttresses, churches could be built higher and the walls could be filled with stained – glass windows. The cathedrals at Chartres and Notre Dame in Paris are examples. Flying buttresses are arches that extend or fly from the upper part of a wall to a pier.

Education was changing also. The monasteries had been centers of learning. Major cathedrals founded schools to train clergy. Now secular clergy would have an education on a par with monks. The universities of Europe originated out of the cathedral schools, and thus owed their creation to the Church. Universities would play a major part in the development of the intellectual, social and public life of Western Christendom. The University of Paris was founded around 1150 and others were founded afterwards.

Bernard of Clairvaux (1090-1153) established the Abbey there and started the Cistercian Reform.

During this time the papacy grew stronger. Popes called and presided over ecumenical councils for the first time. Conflicts continued between the popes and kings but now there was a willingness to settle matters by negotiations rather than by arms.

13th Century

In 1209, Pope Innocent III gave his approval to a rule of life for the order of Friars Minor, which was started by Francis of Assisi (1181-1226). The Second Order of Franciscans, the Poor Clares, was founded in 1212. The Third Order (today The Secular Franciscan Order) was founded by St. Francis in 1221.

Papal approval was also given to a rule of life for the Order of Preachers which was started by the Spaniard, Dominic de Guzman (1170-1221). They are known as Dominicans.

Both orders were mendicants (beggars) and so could identify with the poor. These two orders produced the greatest theologians of that time – the Franciscans, Bonaventure (1221-1274), and the Dominicans, Thomas Aquinas (1225-1274).

A problem arose:

Some began to doubt that the bread and wine are changed into the Body and Blood, Soul and Divinity of Jesus at Mass.

Others said the bread and wine are changed into the Body and Blood, Soul and Divinity of Jesus at Mass.

So, the question was:

What Is The Truth?

The 4th Lateran Council of 1215 formulated, or stated in precise form, the Church's teaching of Transubstantiation; that is, the substance of bread and wine are changed into the Body, Blood, Soul and Divinity of Jesus Christ at Mass. This teaching is in Scripture and was taught and believed in the Catholic Church since the Last Supper. The belief and the teaching is now given a name – Transubstantiation. Just as the Grand Canyon existed before it was given the name Grand Canyon, so too, the changing of the bread and wine into the Body, Blood, Soul and Divinity of Jesus Christ existed before it was given a name.

This Council also instituted the obligation of yearly Confession and Communion at Easter time.

Thomas Aquinas wrote his *Summa Theologiae* which has influenced Western Christian thought up to today.

Scholasticism, a mixture of faith and reason, became the official theological system of the Church.

14th Century

King Phillip IV of France wanted to have more power over the Church in his own country so he tried to undermine the Pope. When Clement V (1305-14) was elected Pope, Philip persuaded him to move from Rome and stay in the French town of Avignon. Clement was weak and gave in. This started the Avignon Papacy which lasted from 1309-1377 – 68 years.

There were disadvantages to the Pope being in Avignon:

1. The Popes were under the influence of the French Kings.
2. To administer the Papal States from a distance was expensive.
3. Popes belong in universal Rome and not in a town in France.

King Philip had the Knights Templar, a crusading order, arrested and took their money. He then had Clement call the ecumenical council of Vienna (1311-1312) which condemned the Templars.

The Black Death spread all over Europe. This Bubonic Plague was spread by infected fleas which bit humans. The plague killed 50 to 80 percent of its victims within 5 or 6 days. The symptoms were fever, swollen and painful joints, swollen lymph nodes (especially in the neck, armpits and groin) and black skin, hence the name "black" death. The Black Death spread to Europe from Asia on merchant ships. From 1347-1351 between 20 and 40 million Europeans died; that is, one-fourth to one-third of the population. It is estimated that 40 percent of the clergy died since they were involved in ministering to the sick. It took 200 years for the population of Europe to recover.

Catholics wanted the Pope back in Rome and Catherine of Sienna (1347-1380) persuaded Pope Gregory XI to return to Rome in 1377.

The cardinals, mostly French, elected an Italian archbishop to be Pope Urban VI (1378-1389). He tried to reform the cardinals, and they did not like it. They then said the Pope's election was a fraud and elected their own pope (an antipope), calling him Clement VII (1378-1394). He stayed at Avignon. This began the Great Western Schism which lasted from 1378-1417, 39 years. There were a number of anti-popes in this period.

An antipope is a pretender to the Papal throne who has been elected, appointed or taken on the title of pope illegitimately. There have been about 39 antipopes from the 3rd century to the 15th century.

These men claimed to be pope, but in fact, were not legitimately elected, or elections were improper. There have been 266 popes, including Peter, to Francis.

15th Century

The Great Western Schism continued. Some cardinals met at Pisa and elected another pope. So, now there were three claiming to be Pope. A Council was held at the Swiss town of Constance (1414-1418) and they elected Martin V. This ended the Schism but brought up another problem – Conciliarism. This claimed that councils had the supreme power in the Church. This theory of conciliarism was never accepted by the popes.

What Is The Truth?

There was a Council at Florence between 1431 and 1449. It decreed that the pope is superior to an ecumenical council and so a council could not depose him. Thus, Conciliarism was rejected. It was also rejected by the First Vatican Council (1869-1870).

Joan of Arc was burned at the stake in 1431 even though she led the French soldiers in victories against the British and helped place Charles VII on the throne in 1429.

Pope Eugene IV died in 1447. Popes who came after him are often referred to as "Renaissance Popes" because their interest was in the arts and not in religion. They interfered in politics and their personal lives left a lot to be desired. Even though their lives were bad they never taught any wrong teachings.

Gutenberg invented movable type printing around 1450. This began a revolution in religion, education, politics, etc.

In 1478 Pope Sixtus IV, at the urging of King Ferdinand of Spain, approved the establishment of the Spanish Inquisition which benefited the crown rather than the Church. Cruelty was exercised and the Holy See repeatedly protested against it, but to no avail.

Columbus discovered America in 1492.

16th Century

Corruption was rampant in the Church. Pope Julius II (1503-1513), who employed Michelangelo to paint the Sistine Chapel, was heavily involved in politics. He personally led papal armies.

The Fifth Lateran Council 1512-1517 did nothing to reform the Church.

The Protestant Revolt & Council of Trent

In 1517, there was an eruption. This event is commonly called the Reformation. The word "revolt" is probably more appropriate. To revolt means to break away or rise against constituted authority. To reform means to improve. Martin Luther sought at first to improve the Catholic Church but broke away or revolted from it instead.

There was a great deal of corruption in the Catholic Church and some little efforts had been made to get rid of the corruption. All came to a head on October 31st, 1517, when Martin Luther (1483-1546) nailed his *Ninety-five Theses* (criticisms of practices in the Church) to the door of the Church in Wittenberg, Germany. He did not intend to break away from the Catholic Church at the time, but he started a revolt in which thousands left the Church, thus beginning the Protestant Revolt. This marked the second big division in Christianity. The term "Protestant" comes from the Second Diet of Speyer in Speyer, Germany, in 1529 when several princes and cities protested a decision involving territory and faith of Catholics and Lutherans. A "Diet" was a meeting of members of the free cities of the Holy Roman Empire in Germany to discuss problems.

In 1521, Luther was excommunicated on more than 40 charges of heresy. Luther died in 1546. He was 63 years old.

The Revolt of the Protestants must be considered to be the greatest catastrophe in the history of the Church because it came from within. In the early 1500 the Catholic Church held a monopoly on religious life and practices in Western Europe. One hundred years later, by the death of Elizabeth I, in 1603, 30% of the faithful had deserted Catholicism and established different sects.

The Protestant Revolt had several effects on the religious, intellectual, political and social life of Europe. It divided Europe into two groups: (1) The Catholics (those who remained in union with the pope) and (2) The Protestants (those who joined different Christian groups after separating themselves from the Catholic Church).

There were many causes for the revolt. Many of those causes dated back to the 14th century.

1. The decline of the authority and prestige of the papacy on account of the Avignon Papacy.
2. The bad popes – Sixtus IV (1471-1484), Alexander VI (1492-1503, the most corrupt of all the popes) and Leo X (1513-1521)
3. The Great Western Schism of 1378-1417
4. The idea of conciliarism.
5. The spread of some heresies
6. Corruption in the Church
7. A weak theology
8. The desire of the rulers in the different countries of Europe to be free of the influence of the Church.
9. A large number of good clergy died during the Black Death (1347-1351). This left a weakness in the instruction of the lay people.

Before the Protestant Revolt there had been efforts made to reform the Church; for example, Catherine of Siena, Thomas More, etc. and the Fifth Lateran Council of 1512. These efforts failed principally on account of the lack of interest and enthusiasm on the part of the papacy.

While thousands were leaving the Church in Europe, millions were coming into it in the New World. In 1531, Our Lady appeared in Guadalupe, Mexico, and in a period of 7 years over 8 million Aztec Indians came into the Church. Missionaries made heroic efforts to spread the Gospel, notably Jesuits, Franciscans and Dominicans who battled for the physical well-being of the native Americans as well as for their spiritual well-being. Missionaries were also active preaching the Gospel in India, Japan, China, Indonesia and the Philippines. There were many martyrs in these lands.

In 1522, Zwingli led the Revolt in Zurich, Switzerland. He died in combat in 1531 at the age of 47.

In 1534, King Henry VIII enacted the Act of Supremacy. Since the Church would not grant him an annulment for his marriage to Catherine of Aragon, he married Anne Boleyn and was excommunicated. He established the Church of England and claimed he had full power over the Church in England. Thomas More and Bishop John Fisher did not accept the oath of supremacy and were executed in 1535. Henry died in 1547 after the age of 56.

From 1555 to 1564, John Calvin led the Revolt in Switzerland.

In 1534, an outstanding pope began the renewal of the Church. He was Paul III (1534-1549). He appointed good bishops and approved the establishment of the Society of Jesus, founded by the Spaniard, Ignatius of Loyola (1491-1556). The Jesuits did a great deal to renew the Church through mission work, education and preaching. Paul III called the Council of Trent (1545-1563) which stated clearly the teaching of the Catholic Church on several issues. It taught on the sacraments, emphasized the necessity of seminaries, defined the canon of the Bible, belief in purgatory, etc. It had a catechism published. Trent & Vatican II are considered to be the greatest ecumenical councils held in the West.

This was also an Age of Missions. There was a New World in which to preach the Gospel. Jesuits, Franciscans, Dominicans and others heeded the call to go to the missions. Francis Xavier, S.J. (Jesuit), went to India, Sri Lanka and Japan and died off the coast of China in 1552. Juniper Serra, O.F.M. (Franciscan), established missions up and down the coast of California.

The missionary work of the Church was often hindered by the cruel acts of the Spanish conquistadores towards the native peoples. Fr. Bartolome de las Casas (1484-1566) worked among the native peoples from 1514 until his death. He stood up for their rights and, with the help of other missionaries, persuaded the popes and Spanish rulers that the native peoples had rights. A large portion of South America had been evangelized, and progress was being made in North America. Eusebio Kino, S.J. worked in Baja California and Arizona until his death in 1711. Several were martyred, such as Jean de Brebeuf and Isaac Jogues. This was in upstate New York and S.E. Canada between 1642 and 1649. Kateri Tekakwitha, Lily of the Mohawks, was brought into the Church by the Jesuits at this time.

The oldest Christian community in the United States was founded by the Spaniards at St. Augustine, Florida, in 1565.

The Battle of Lepanto, one of the most important naval battles in human history, took place in 1571. The outnumbered Catholic fleet defeated the Turks and saved Europe from being taken over by the Muslims. The battle lasted 5 hours. The Christians had just over 200 boats with 80,000 men. The Turks had 225 galleys (ships) and 50 boats with 120,000 men. Statistics were: Christian deaths 9,000 men; Turkish deaths 12,000 men; 117 Turkish galleys captured; 12,000 galley slaves freed. The Christians prayed the rosary throughout the night on the night before the battle. Pope Pius V prayed the rosary all day on the day of the battle, hence Pope Pius V attributed the victory to the Blessed Virgin Mary, naming the day a feast day of Our Lady of Victory (later called Our Lady of the Rosary). Pope Pius V was a Dominican and wore the Dominican white habit and this is why the popes since then have worn a white habit.

***JESUS CHRIST
DID NOT
ESTABLISH THE
CHRISTIAN RELIGION.
JESUS CHRIST
ESTABLISHED
ONE CHURCH.***

"You are Peter, and upon this rock I will build my church."
Matthew 16:18

There are many teachings in Christianity that
contradict each other.
These could not have come from Jesus because
He is Truth and does not contradict Himself.

17th Century

In this century, the Catholic Monarchs as usual did not want the popes to interfere in their affairs in Europe. However, the Pope was powerful in Italy. Urban VIII (1623-1644) employed Bernini to add the famous baldachino with its twisting pillars to St. Peter's Basilica. Urban VIII also condemned Galileo (1564-1642) for supporting the theory of Nicholas Copernicus (1473-1543), a Polish cathedral canon (one who advises the bishop), which said that the planets revolve around the sun. The case against Galileo was closed in his favor in 1992.

The French King, Louis XIV (1643-1715) wanted to control the French Church. The Pope, Innocent XI (1676-1689), resisted his efforts.

18th Century

The Catholic monarchs continued to try to control the Church in their countries and to lessen the pope's right to interfere in political issues.

The monarchs hated the Jesuits (Society of Jesus) because:

1. The Jesuits had criticized the monarchs for their actions in the Americas, and
2. The Jesuits had always remained loyal to the popes.

So, in 1773 a weak-willed Clement XIV dissolved the Jesuits. They were reinstated 41 years later in 1814 by Pope Pius VII, a Benedictine.

Freemasonry was condemned by Pope Clement XII in 1738. Catholics were forbidden to join the Masons under penalty of excommunication. This prohibition was repeated by Benedict XIV in 1751 and by later popes.

The Age of Enlightenment or Reason arrived in Europe in the 18th century. European intellectuals set up Reason as the final authority on all matters, thus pushing aside scripture and doctrine. Voltaire was one of the leaders. Since that time the most influential thinkers in the West have been atheists or secularists. Religious intellectuals have been cast aside. This was a blow to the Church's influence.

The French Revolution began in 1789. Church property was seized, priests, religious and lay persons loyal to the Pope were persecuted and thousands were martyred. Napoleon invaded the Papal States in 1796. Papal States were lands donated by wealthy Catholics to the Church over many centuries. The French monarchy was overthrown, attempts were made to de-Christianize France and establish a new religion, Rome was occupied by French troops and Pope Pius VI (1775-1799) was forced to go to France in 1798, and died there in 1799.

Religious freedom in the United States was guaranteed under the First Amendment to the Constitution.

19th Century

Napoleon had Pope Pius VII (1800-1823) arrested in 1809 and brought to France. The Pope refused to cooperate with Napoleon who wanted to bring the Church in France under his control. Pius VII remained in France until the emperor's fall in 1814.

Pope Pius VII restored the Jesuits, or the Society of Jesus. They had been suppressed in 1773.

Missionary efforts continued and the Pope reestablished the Congregation for the Propagation of the Faith in 1820 (originally founded in 1622 by Pope Gregory XV) in order to give the missionary efforts more strength.

The Church had been fiercely persecuted in China. Thousands were martyred. The persecution ended in 1820. However, communication with the West remained cut off until about 1834. Zealous missionary efforts began again in China in 1842.

The Catholic Emancipation Act in England in 1829 freed the Catholics in England and Ireland from most of the civil disabilities which had been imposed on them during the time of Henry VIII.

The Oxford Movement began in 1833. Many Church of England members, including John Henry Newman (1801-1890) converted to the Catholic Church.

The Society of St. Vincent De Paul was founded in France by Frederick Ozanam. Its purpose was to do works of charity.

Vatican Council I was held in 1869-1870. It defined the primacy of the Pope and papal infallibility; that is, the Pope can not make a mistake when teaching faith or morals, ex cathedra or from the chair. He is said to speak ex cathedra when he exercises his office as the shepherd and teacher of all Christians in virtue of his supreme apostolic authority and defines a doctrine concerning faith or morals to be held by the whole Church. He has to make it clear that he is teaching ex cathedra or from the chair. The chair being the symbol of the seat of teaching. It does not mean that he is free from sin, but that he is teaching the truth. This has only been done twice – once in 1854, when the Pope declared the Immaculate Conception of the Blessed Virgin Mary; that is, that she was conceived free from Original Sin, and secondly, in 1950, when the Pope declared the Assumption of the Blessed Virgin Mary; that is, that she was carried body and soul into heaven.

Leo XIII was elected pope (1878-1903). His encyclical, *Rerum Novarum*, defended the rights of workers. He emphasized scripture studies and scholastic philosophy.

The Catholic Church was growing in the United States because of the work of the missionaries and Catholic immigration from Germany, Ireland, Southern and Eastern Europe.

From the 1850's up to today there has been a strong emphasis on devotion to the Blessed Virgin Mary.

1. Pope Pius IX proclaimed the dogma of the Immaculate Conception on December 8, 1854. This means that Mary was conceived free from Original Sin.
2. The Blessed Virgin Mary appeared to Bernadette Soubirous at Lourdes in France in 1858. Many miracles were reported to have occurred there through the years.
3. In 1879, Our Lady appeared in Knock, Ireland, to several people of different ages, and 15 official witnesses gave testimony.
4. Our Lady appeared to 3 children at Fatima, Portugal, and 70,000 to 100,000 people saw the Miracle of the Sun on October 13, 1917. The sun danced and appeared to come down toward the earth and go back into the heavens, as reported in the secular newspapers at that time.
5. In 1950, the Pope proclaimed the Assumption of the Blessed Virgin Mary or that Mary was carried body and soul into heaven.
6. In 1981, Our Lady appeared in Kibeho in Rwanda, Africa, to 3 children.
7. In 1981, Our Lady reportedly appeared to 6 children, and continues to appear to some of them, in Medjugorje, the former Yugoslovia.

This devotion to Mary has given rise to new religious orders which were named for her. The Legion of Mary, which has done wonderful work in regard to evangelization, was established in 1921 by Frank Duff. Lay sodalities were also founded.

The Papal States were seized by King Victor Emmanuel II in 1870 after Napoleon III fell. Napoleon III had protected the Papal States.

Charles Darwin, who proposed a theory of evolution, died in 1882.

The Knights of Columbus was started by Fr. Michael J. McGivney in 1882, at St. Mary's Church in New Haven, Connecticut. This is a major force as a Catholic fraternal investment and insurance society serving the interests of Church and society.

20th Century

Because of persecution in France, thousands of priests and religious had to leave the country. Schools were closed. Church property was seized.

Pope Pius X (1903-14) encouraged Catholics to receive Holy Communion often, and children could begin to receive Holy Communion at the age of reason or 7 years.

World War I raged from 1914 to 1918. Pope Pius X, who had worked for peace, died as the War began. Throughout the war the Church tried to bring peace, comfort, shelter and spiritual and material help to victims. Pope Benedict XV offered to be a mediator in those different times, but was turned down.

Laws were passed in Mexico which resulted in terrible persecution of the Church in the 1920's and 1930's.

In 1917, the Bolsheviks seized power and set up a communist dictatorship which would persecute the Church and others.

A new Code of Canon Law was put into effect in 1918.

Pope Pius XI (1922-1939) signed the Lateran Treaty in 1929 setting up the present state of Vatican City, which is the smallest sovereign state in the world, comprising 108.7 acres. He had to deal with three dictators – Mussolini in Italy, Stalin in Russia and Hitler in Germany. He tried to negotiate with them to preserve rights for the Church. He also spoke directly to the people of the world through a number of encyclicals.

In 1933, Adolph Hitler came to power in Germany. Two of his goals were, first, to eliminate the Jews and others in his way. He had 5 to 6 million Jews killed and 11 to 13 million other peoples killed. The second goal was to control a single national church. He persecuted the Church.

In 1936-1939, Civil War in Spain resulted in many priests, religious and lay people being killed.

Through World War II (1939-1945), Pope Pius XII (1939-1958) worked tirelessly to bring peace. He opened monasteries and convents which had been closed to the public for hundreds of years so that the Jews could escape the Nazi persecution. In this way he saved thousands of Jews. The chief Rabbi of Rome, Zolli, was so impressed with the efforts of Pope Pius XII on behalf of his people that he converted to Catholicism in 1945 and took the name Eugenio (the Pope's first name). Pope Pius XII also condemned communism.

In 1957, in China the Patriotic Association of Chinese Catholics was set up in opposition to the Church in union with the Pope.

In 1940, religious persecution by the communists started and reached its height after World War II. Communism spread across Eastern Europe, China, North Korea and North Vietnam. Thousands were martyred for the faith.

Pope John XXIII (1958-1963) called the Second Ecumenical Council of the Vatican (1962-1965).

Pope Paul VI (1963-1978) tried to bring about the renewal called for by Vatican II.

Pope John Paul II (1978-2005) was the first non-Italian pope in 450 years. He traveled a great deal, making him the most traveled pope in history and the most recognized leader in the entire world. He worked zealously to put the teachings of Vatican II into effect. He restored a great deal of the Church's organization and vitality which had been lost during the tumultuous years after Vatican II. He promoted Christian unity and ecumenism. He canonized and beatified more men and women than all of his predecessors combined. He revised the Code of Canon Law in1983 and approved the Catechism of the Catholic Church in 1992. Towards the end of his life, he suffered a great deal from declining health and died on April 2nd 2005.

21st Century

Pope Benedict XVI (2005-2013) reached out to bring unity among Christians, co-operation with other religions, reconciliation with theologians, wrote extensively about Jesus of Nazareth, pleaded for peace throughout the world, emphasized Religious Liberty and the rights of the human being.

Pope Francis (2013-) is reaching out to the poor, promoting peace and reconciliation, and reorganizing the Vatican.

Time-Line of the History of the Catholic Church

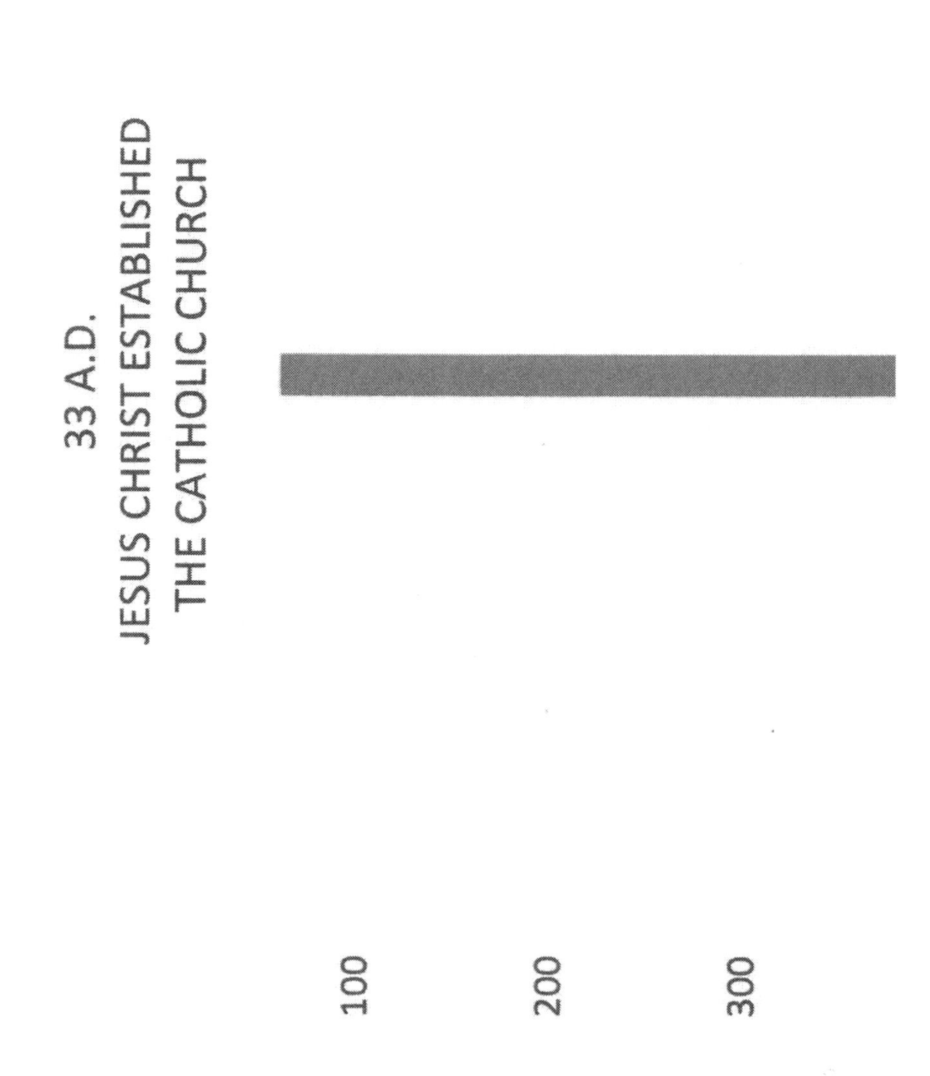

400

500

600

700

Time-Line of the History of the Catholic Church

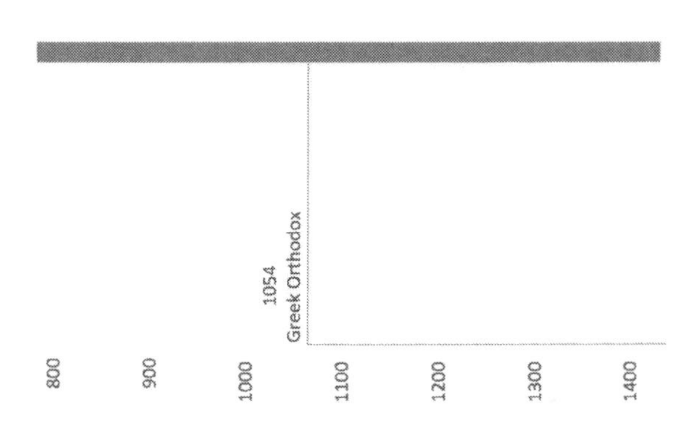

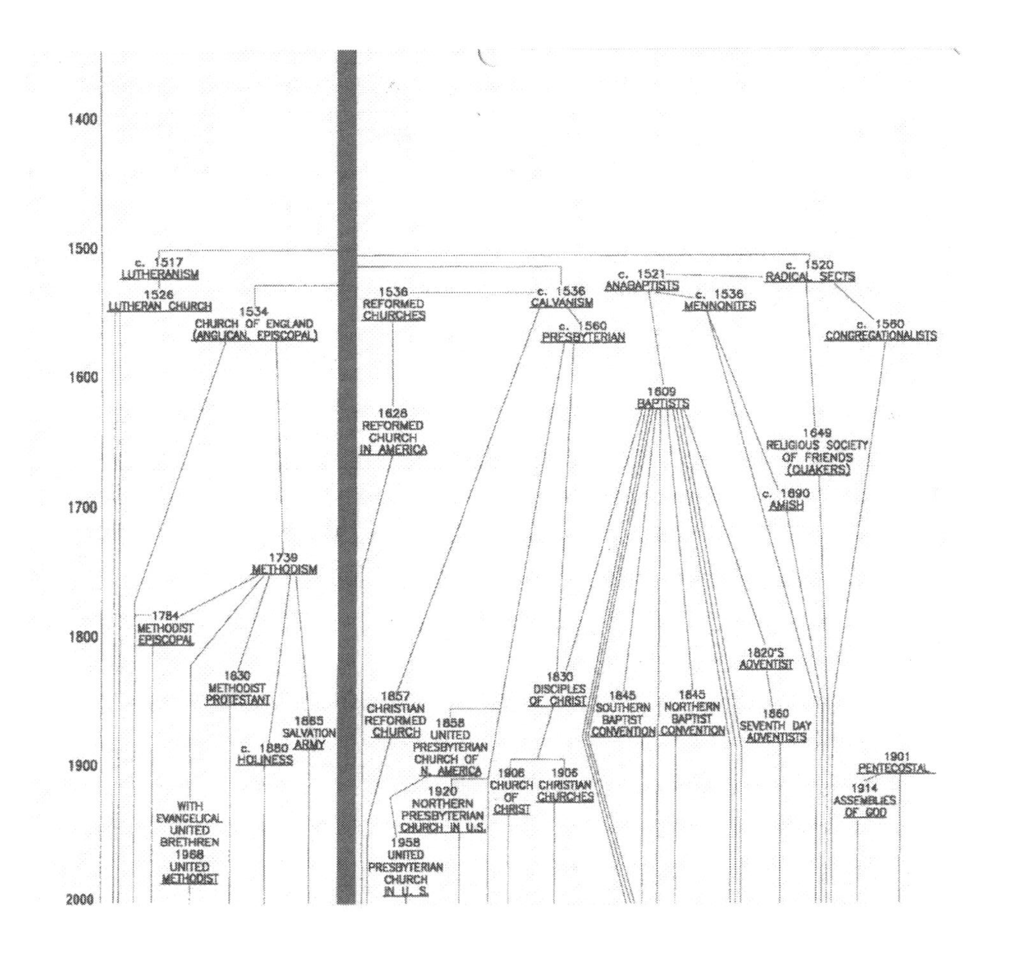
1400
1500
1600
1700
1800
1900
2000
c. 1517 LUTHERANISM
1526 LUTHERAN CHURCH
1534 CHURCH OF ENGLAND (ANGLICAN, EPISCOPAL)
1739 METHODISM
1784 METHODIST EPISCOPAL
1830 METHODIST PROTESTANT
1865 SALVATION ARMY
c. 1880 HOLINESS
WITH EVANGELICAL UNITED BRETHREN 1968 UNITED METHODIST
1536 REFORMED CHURCHES
1628 REFORMED CHURCH IN AMERICA
c. 1536 CALVANISM
c. 1560 PRESBYTERIAN
1857 CHRISTIAN REFORMED CHURCH
1858 UNITED PRESBYTERIAN CHURCH OF N. AMERICA
1920 NORTHERN PRESBYTERIAN CHURCH IN U.S.
1958 UNITED PRESBYTERIAN CHURCH IN U. S.
1830 DISCIPLES OF CHRIST
1906 CHURCH OF CHRIST
1906 CHRISTIAN CHURCHES
c. 1521 ANABAPTISTS
1609 BAPTISTS
1845 SOUTHERN BAPTIST CONVENTION
1845 NORTHERN BAPTIST CONVENTION
c. 1536 MENNONITES
1820'S ADVENTIST
1860 SEVENTH DAY ADVENTISTS
c. 1520 RADICAL SECTS
c. 1580 CONGREGATIONALISTS
1649 RELIGIOUS SOCIETY OF FRIENDS (QUAKERS)
c. 1690 AMISH
1901 PENTECOSTAL
1914 ASSEMBLIES OF GOD

Origin of Well-Known Non-Christian Churches and Religions

RELIGION	FOUNDER	YEAR	PLACE
Ancestor Worship	Evolved over several centuries		China
Bahaism	Mirza Ali Muhammad	1850 A.D.	Iran
Bilalians (Black Muslims)	Timothy Drew (aka Nobel Drew Ali)	1910's A.D.	Newark, NJ
Buddhism	Siddhartha Gautama	c. 500 B.C.	India
Zen Buddhism	Bodhidharma	520 B.C.	China
Confucianism	Confucius	c. 500 B.C.	China
Hinduism	Vedas Writings	c. 500 B.C.	India
Hare Krishnas (Iskon) (Hinduism)	Swami Prabhupada	1965 A.D.	New York
Islam (Muslims)	Mohammed	622 A.D.	Medina, Saudi Arabia
Jehovah Witness	Charles Taze Russell	1879 A.D.	Pittsburgh, PA
Judaism	**God**	**c. 1850 B.C.**	**Ur, Babylonia**
Mormon (Latter-day Saints)	Joseph Smith	1829 A.D.	New York
Radio Church of God (Worldwide Church of God)	Herbert W. Armstrong	1934 A.D.	U.S.A.
Rosicrucian	H. Spencer Lewis	1915 A.D.	New York
Shintoism	Evolved over several centuries		Japan
Spiritualism	Margaret and Kate Fox	1848 A.D.	New York
Taoism	Lao-Tse	c. 580 B.C.	China
Theosophy	Helena Petrovna Blavatsky	1875 A.D.	New York
Transcendental Meditation (Hinduism)	Maharishi Yogi	1970 A.D.	India
Unification Church	Sun Myung Moon	1945 A.D.	Korea
Unitarianism	Francis David	1550's A.D.	Transylvania
Universalism	James Relly	1700'S A.D.	England

Origin of Well-Known Non-Christian Churches and Religions - Con't

RELIGION	FOUNDER	YEAR	PLACE
Unitarian-Universalist	From Unit. & Univ. Religions	1961 A.D.	U.S.A.
Zoroasterism	Zoroaster compiled ancient teaching	1000-600 B.C.	Iran

Origin of Well-Known Christian Churches

CHURCH	FOUNDER	YEAR	PLACE
Catholic	**Jesus Christ**	**A.D. 33**	**Palestine**
Adventist	William Miller	c. 1820	U.S.A.
Amish	Jacob Amman	c.1600	Switzerland
Assemblies of God	From Pentecostalism	1914	Hot Springs, AR
Baptist	John Smyth	1609	Holland
Christadelphian (Brethren of Christ)	John Thomas	c.1844	Richmond, VA
Christian Scientist	Mary Baker Eddy	1879	Boston
Church of Christ (Disciples of Christ)	Thomas Campbell	c. 1827	Kentucky
Church of God	From different religious bodies	end of the 19th cen.	U.S.A.
Church of God in Christ	Largest of Church of God	1895	Arkansas
Church of Nazarene	from different religious bodies	1908	Pilot Point, TX
Congregational	Robert Brown	1600	England
Congregationalist	Pilgrims and Puritans	1648	Massachusetts
Episcopal (Anglican, Church of England)	Henry VIII	1534	England
Four Square Gospel	Aimee Semple McPherson	1927	Los Angeles, CA
Holiness	From Methodism	1867	U.S.A.
Lutheran	Martin Luther	1517	Germany
Mennonite	Menno Simons	c.1536	Switzerland

Origin of Well-Known Christian Churches - Con't

CHURCH	FOUNDER	YEAR	PLACE
Methodist	John Wesley	1739	England
Methodist Episcopal	60 Preachers	1784	Baltimore, MD
Methodist Protestant	Methodism	1830	U.S.A.
Pentecostal	Charles F. Parkham	1901	Topeka, KS
Presbyterian	John Knox	1560	Scotland
Quaker (Religious Society of Friends)	George Fox	1649	England
Salvation Army	William Booth	1865	London
Seventh Day Adventist	Ellen Harmon White	1844	Washington, NH
Seventh Day Baptist	Stephen Mumford	1672	Newport, RI
United Church of Christ	From Reformed & Congregationalist Churches	1961	Philadelphia, PA
United Methodist	From Methodist & Evangelical United Brethren Churches	1968	Dallas, TX

So that they may all be one, as you, Father, are in me and I in you, that they also may be in us, that the world may believe that you sent me. Jn 17:21

One Lord, one faith, one baptism; God and Father of all, who is over all and through all and in all. Eph 4:5-6

Part Two – The Bible

Introduction

> *All Sacred Scripture is but one book, and this one book is Christ, because all divine Scripture speaks of Christ, and all divine Scripture is fulfilled in Christ.*
>
> (Hugh of St. Victor, CCC 134)

No book has been so widely spread, or has exercised such a far-reaching influence on the religion, morality and civilization of mankind as the Bible. It was the first book to be printed after printing was invented in 1450. It is the world's most popular book and is now available in over 2,300 languages. In 1804 the Bible appeared in only 67 translations. That grew to 500 by the end of the 19th century and double that number 50 years ago. Still, there is much more work to be done. The world has more than 6,500 recorded languages.

All Christians believe that the Bible is the Word of God. A look at its history is very helpful. For instance, where did the Bible come from? Where did the Bible get its name? Who wrote the Bible? Who put the Bible together? Millions believe that the Bible is the Word of God, but who had the authority to say that the Bible is the Word of God in the first place?

The word "Bible" comes from the Greek "biblion" which is "book" or "ta biblia" which is "the books." The Bible is regarded as a single book. In fact, it is a sacred library of books. This collection of books had become of such great importance to the humanities and religion that it became known in Western Civilization as "The Book" or "The Book of Books" or "The Bible." The Bible is about God revealing Himself to His people, the Jewish people first, then revealing Himself to all people in His Son, Jesus Christ. The entire Bible is the story of the love which God has for mankind whom He created in His own image and likeness. The Old

Testament gives us images of Israel as the Bride of the Lord and the New Testament gives us images of the Church as the Bride of Christ. Throughout the entire Bible the love of God is ALWAYS steadfast. The Bible reveals the Truth which we need to know for salvation. It tells us (1) Who God is, and (2) How He wants us to live. "All Sacred Scripture is but one book, and this one book is Christ, because all divine Scripture speaks of Christ, and all divine Scripture is fulfilled in Christ," said Hugh of St. Victor (CCC 134).

Who wrote the Bible?

God is the author of the Bible. So, the Bible is not only about God, it is also by Him. The Bible is God's Love Letter to His people. It is God's Gift to us. God utilized many men to write the Bible. These human authors were inspired by the Holy Spirit; that is, the Holy Spirit breathed into them the ideas which He wanted expressed, and they expressed these ideas in their own way and in their own language at that time. This is called Inspiration. It was not the intention of the human authors to write a book that would be entered into "The Bible," as we know it. The whole thrust was to preserve the traditions of how God dealt with His people. The authors of the books did not know that God was inspiring them to write. It was only over time that the Church recognized which writings were inspired.

In What Language Was the Bible Written?

The languages in which the books of the Bible were written are Hebrew, Aramaic and Greek. Most of the Old Testament books were written in Hebrew. Parts of Daniel, Ezra, Jeremiah, Esther and probably Tobit and Judith were written in Aramaic (the language spoken by Jesus which was related to Hebrew and popular in Palestine during His time). The Book of Wisdom, 1st and 2nd Maccabees and all the books of the New Testament were written in Greek. Some say Matthew wrote a shorter Gospel in Aramaic, but it no longer exists.

When Was the Bible Written?

It took a long time to write it – about 1,500 years – from approximately 1450 B.C. to 100 A.D.

The Different Kinds of Writing in the Bible

We must remember the Bible is NOT a single book. It is a LIBRARY of sacred books. There are many different kinds of writings in these books; for example, history, prose, proverbs, parables, prophecy, prayers, poetry, (narrative hymns), legends, legal documents, letters, sermons, songs, stories, etc. This is called Literary Form.

How is the Bible Divided?

The Bible is divided into the Old Testament (containing 46 books), and the New Testament (containing 27 books). Total 73 books.

> *God wisely arranged that the New Testament be hidden in the Old, and that the Old Testament be made perfect in the New.*
>
> (St. Augustine)

What is the Old Testament and the New Testament About?

The word testament means covenant. A covenant is a kinship bond, or a bond of family relationship. It is between two parties. Obligations or conditions are attached to it. The parties are legally bound by an oath. It is often sealed with blood.

A person needs to understand the Old Testament in order to understand the New Testament.

The Old Testament, or Old Covenant, involves the family bond between God and the Israelites wherein He would be their God, and they would be His people (Exodus 24:1-8). Moses referred to the blood of the covenant which the Lord made with the people according to His Word (Exodus 24:8). The Old Covenant was sealed with the blood of animals and an oath. The New Testament (a title given to it by St. Clement of Alexandria around 215 A.D.), or New Covenant, involves the fulfillment of the Old Covenant by a New Covenant with God. Jeremiah 31:33 says that God said He would place His Law within the hearts of His people. In Luke's Gospel 22:20, Jesus said, *"This cup is the new covenant in My blood, which is shed for you."*. The New Covenant was sealed with the

Blood of Jesus Christ and the promise made at baptism which is belief in God the Father, belief in Jesus Christ, His only Son, belief in the Holy Spirit and the Holy Catholic Church.

The division of the Bible into chapters was a result of work done by Stephen Langton (d. 1228), a professor at the University of Paris, who later became the Archbishop of Canterbury in England. Father Santes Pagninus, a Dominican priest, divided the Old Testament chapters into verses in 1528, and Robert Etienne, a printer in Paris, did the same for the New Testament in 1551.

How the Bible Developed

It developed or came together in three stages.

1. **Oral Stage** – Stories handed down through the generations by word of mouth (almost all of the Book of Genesis is from oral accounts, or what we call Tradition). The more important stories were memorized and told on special occasions.
2. **Writing Stage** – As time went on, people began to write things down. Writing was difficult, and very few people could read. For hundreds of years both Oral Tradition and the written word existed side by side. Some parts of the Bible were written to meet a particular need of the community, Jewish or Christian. Not all Oral Traditions were written down.
3. **Editing Stage** – Material was chosen which best represented the religious traditions of the people. The oral and written accounts could have differed slightly, so editing was done to bring unity between the two. The contents of the Bible came from this last stage. These three stages of development existed for the most part simultaneously, though the Oral Stage came first and the Editing Stage came last.

The Old Testament is Organized Under Three Major Headings:

1. **The Law** – this is the first in importance and consists of the first five books. It is sometimes called the Torah, or the Pentateuch.

2. **The Prophets** – consisting of the preaching attributed to the prophets and their writings and the Books of Joshua, Judges, Samuel and Kings.
3. **The Writings** – this is the remainder of the Old Testament. The Old Testament is preparation for the coming of the Messiah.

Where Are the Original Manuscripts of the Bible?

The original manuscripts of the Bible no longer exist. We have copies of copies. The materials on which the books of the Bible were originally written were stone (probably), papyrus, parchment and vellum.

Papyrus – (from which we get the word "paper") was developed by the Egyptians about 2,500 B.C. Papyrus was a thin paper-like product which was made from reeds that grew mostly in the Nile Delta. The reeds were cut in long strips, arranged crosswise in two or three layers, soaked in water and pressed into a smooth surface. Then they joined several of these together and rolled them on a rod to make something like a scroll. This material was used by ancient Egyptians, Greeks, and Romans as a writing material, especially between the 4th century B.C. and the 4th century A.D. They inscribed their symbols on these. Symbols for the spoken words were developed about 6,000 years ago.

About 105 A.D., the Chinese invented paper, but it was not introduced into the Western world until about 700 A.D. It was more than 700 years later (1450 A.D.) that Johann Gutenberg invented printing.

Parchment is sheepskin, and **vellum** is calfskin. These are materials of finer quality than papyrus. In the 4th century A.D., parchment displaced papyrus in common use. It remained the usual material of which books were made until the invention of printing in 1450 A.D. The oldest Old Testament copies that we have are the Dead Sea Scrolls.

Among the Dead Sea Scrolls is a complete copy of Isaiah, and pieces of almost all the Old Testament books. These scrolls date from the 2nd century B.C. to the 2nd century A.D.

The earliest entire copy of the New Testament that we have, which is written on parchment, is called the Codex Sinaiticus. It dates from the 4th century A.D. Manuscripts disintegrated rather quickly. Time, humidity, and people destroyed them. The Holy Land was a land of many battles. Manuscripts were destroyed during these battles. Deliberate attempts were made to destroy manuscripts. This was done even in Old Testament times. Around 175 B.C. Antiochus IV sent his soldiers to find and destroy the Jewish scriptures. For almost 1,000 years monks made copies of the Bible by hand. When finished, they would throw away the older copies.

Writings of Sacred Scripture Before Christ

These writings make up the Old Testament today.

Approximately 1450 B.C.: in Deuteronomy 31:24-26 we read that Moses had finished writing the Law on a scroll. He gave the Levites, who dealt with matters of worship and religious instruction, the order to place the scroll beside the Ark of the Covenant. Since the Ark was the symbol of God's presence and the most sacred item they had, to put this scroll beside it indicated that the scroll was sacred too. Moses wrote the Law and gave it to the elders and priests. It was probably written on a scroll or stone tablets, maybe on skins, which had been dried out, or written on papyrus.

1420 B. C.: Joshua 8: 30-35. Joshua inscribed upon the stones a copy of the law written by Moses.

In Joshua 24:26, Joshua recorded a covenant with the people in the Book of the Law of God. He then took a large stone and set it there under the oak that was the sanctuary of the Lord. It was set up in the sanctuary of the Lord, beside the Ark, to show that this writing was regarded as sacred.

Approximately 590 B.C.: In Jeremiah 30:1-2, the Lord told Jeremiah to write all the words He had spoken to him in a book.

c. 450 B.C.: Nehemiah 8:1-8, Ezra read the law to the people who stood, bowed down and prostrated themselves before the Lord, their faces to the ground. Again, this shows the reverence the people had for the sacred writings.

It is said that Nehemiah began to put together a library of the sacred books.

From 1450 B.C. to the 5th century B.C. the sacred writings were mostly in Hebrew.

The Septuagint

In the 4th century B.C., Alexander the Great conquered the known world. He spread the Greek language and Greek culture. This gave rise to the most ancient and famous translation of the Hebrew sacred books - the *Septuagint* which is the Old Testament today.

Around 280 B.C., a translation of the sacred writings was made from Hebrew to Greek. This translation is called the *Septuagint* because it comes from the Latin word for seventy, septuaginta. Seventy scholars were hired to translate the writings.

Eusebius, in Book 5 of his "Church History," tells us that Ptolemy, King of Egypt, had set up a magnificent library in Alexandria, Egypt, and he wanted to add the Hebrew sacred writings to the thousands and thousands of books in it. (Unfortunately, this library was destroyed by the Second Muslim Caliph, Umar ibn al-Khattab, in the 7th century A.D.) Also, the Jews who had been captured in 320 B.C. and brought to Alexandria and the surrounding area (about 200,000 people) wanted to have a Greek translation of their sacred writings. They were gradually losing all knowledge of their Hebrew mother tongue and adopting the Greek language. Seventy elders, who were experts in Hebrew and Greek, were sent to translate the sacred writings. Ptolemy separated the experts to ensure that there would be no secrecy or trickery involved in the translation. All seventy independently wrote the exact same translation. The Jews accepted the Septuagint translation right away because they realized that this was a miracle – all seventy translated in the same words independently of each other. The first century Jewish historian, Josephus, regarded this incident as history. The name Septuagint applied to the Books of Moses (the first five books of the Old Testament), but was afterwards extended to include the other books of the Old Testament as they were translated during the next 100 years. This included the **Seven Books** which are in the Catholic Bible but not in the Protestant Bible.

Many Greek-speaking non-Jews read this Greek translation and gained a knowledge of how God was dealing with His people and consequently they were prepared to accept the Gospel when it was later preached to them. (More on the **Seven Books** later.)

The *Septuagint* is by far the most important version of the Sacred Writings before the time of Christ. It was the version used by the Hebrews outside of Palestine at the time of Christ and by some inside of Palestine.

Sacred Writings at the Time of Jesus

Jesus read from the Prophet Isaiah (Luke 4: 14-21). On the Road to Emmaus, He opened the minds of the disciples to the scriptures (Luke 24:13-35). So, Jesus did accept the scriptures of Israel but He did not say what was inspired and what was not.

At the time of Jesus there were 3 groups with different sets of Sacred Writings:

1. **The Sadducees** – They accepted as inspired only the 5 Books of Moses (Law, Pentateuch, Torah).
2. **The Pharisees** – Josephus, an historian who wrote the history of the Jews in over 20 volumes around 93 to 94 A.D. called *Antiquities of the Jews,* mentioned that they accepted 22 books.
3. **The Essenes** – They had a sacred library which we call "The Dead Sea Scrolls." These were discovered in 1947 in a cave in Qumran. In the sacred library of the Essenes was a full scroll, 30' long, of the Book of Isaiah which is 1,000 years older than any copy we already had. There were copies of Genesis, Exodus, Leviticus, Deuteronomy, Jeremiah, and copies of every book of the Jewish Old Testament, except Esther. Some pieces of books in the Catholic Old Testament were found – Sirach, Tobit, etc. So, they read the **Seven Books** also. These are the oldest copies of the Old Testament that we now possess.

In Jesus' time, the canon of the Hebrew Scriptures was not yet set.

Putting the Bible Together

Why were the Gospels not written when Jesus was alive, or at least shortly after He ascended into heaven?

1. There were no reporters around at the time.
2. There was no rush to write because Jesus' followers thought that He was coming back soon.
3. Very few people were able to read or write. Jesus did not tell His Apostles to "Go, write a book." He said, "Go TEACH all nations." He left a group of men to hand on His message. They did this in the Bible, Liturgy, the Creed, Church Councils, teaching of the early Fathers, and the teaching authority of the bishops, especially the Pope; that is, Sacred Tradition.
4. The followers of Jesus decided to write when they finally realized that eye-witnesses to the events in Jesus' life were dying and, if they did not write, the truth may not be passed on to future generations.

The Four Gospels

The word gospel comes from an Anglo-Saxon word, and means good news. It means the good news of salvation proclaimed by Christ and the Church, and given to us in written form by Matthew, Mark, Luke and John. Bible Scholars of every persuasion agree that Mark was written between 65 and 70 A.D., Matthew and Luke in the 80's, and John in the 90's.

Fathers of the Church

The Fathers of the Church were men who were recognized for their holiness of life, orthodoxy toward doctrine, approval of the Church and antiquity. Some of these men were Paul, Polycarp, Irenaeus, Clement of Alexandria and Origen. The Fathers of the Church did not quote writings when they were not certain as to who the author was and also if the writings were not in line with the teaching of the Apostles. There were several writings around in the early Church. There were at least 39 Gospels; at least 16 Acts of the Apostles; at least 7 Books of Revelation;

at least 39 Epistles or Letters; and at least 20 other writings. There were some writings that the Fathers accepted – the 4 Gospels, Acts of the Apostles, Epistles of Paul. There were disputes about other writings; for example, Epistle of James, Jude, Letter of Clement of Rome, third Successor of Peter, etc. Some rejected the Apocalypse of John, Didache, etc. Others were rejected outright; for example, Gospel of Peter, Gospel of Thomas, etc.

Some writings were recognized as heretical. So, there was disagreement, even among the Fathers of the Church, about the canon of the New Testament or what books were inspired and should be included in the Canon. The Bible does not tell us which ancient Jewish and Christian writings are inspired by God nor does it give us the list of all the books which are to be in the Bible.

So, What Is The Truth?

> The Father will give you another Advocate, the Spirit of Truth.
> Jn 14:16

Who Decided What Books Were To Make Up the Canon of The Old Testament and the Canon of the New Testament?

Who decided what Books were inspired and were, therefore, teaching the truth?

The Catholic Church decided.

"Canon" is Greek for a measuring rod. Scripture serves as a measuring rod for the truth – a standard against which we can measure our faith and conduct. A book is canonical because it is inspired. An Inspired Book is a book written by God Who utilizes a human being to write it. A Canonical Book is a book recognized by the Church as inspired and proposed to the faithful as the Word of God and a source of revealed doctrine.

In Jesus' time, there was no canon of Sacred Scripture. Some say that the Canon of the Old Testament was settled at the Council of Jamnia in 90 A.D. However, there is no historical evidence that this council or meeting of rabbis ever took place. Even if it did take place the decision of the rabbis, who did not believe in Jesus Christ, would have no bearing on the Christian community. The Holy Spirit guided the Church. The living Church gradually discovered which of the many writings of very early Christianity were to be in the "canon." Origen (d 254) was the first person to use the term "canon" in reference to scripture, but St. Athanasius (d 373) first used the phrase "canonized books". He was the first to list the 27 Books of the New Testament as we have them today in his Letter, *39th Festal Letter,* of 367.

1. The **Council of Rome**, in 382, was called together by Pope Damasus I (366-384) to, among other things, take up this issue of the canon of scripture. The Council declared that there were 46 books in the Old Testament and 27 in the New Testament. The Council gives a list of the entire Old Testament and New Testament books as we have in the Catholic Bible today. The Council said, "The Canon of the New Testament ends here." In the late 300's and 400's the ordinary people spoke Latin, so Pope Damasus I, now that the canon was decided upon, commissioned St. Jerome, the most learned biblical scholar of his day, to translate the Bible from the original languages into the everyday language of the "common people" (in Latin, "vulgus"). Hence the name *Vulgate.* The *Vulgate* has been the Catholic Church's official Latin text of the Bible up to today. It was revised in 1986. Some of the Fathers of the Church may not have agreed with the list of the books which made up the Canon but they considered the issue to be settled since "Rome had spoken" through the Council of Rome.

   Other councils restated the Council of Rome's list of inspired writings that we have in the Catholic Bible today.
2. **Council of Hippo** in North Africa in 393 A.D.
3. **Council of Carthage** in North Africa in 397 A.D.
4. **Pope Innocent I** wrote to Bishop Exsuperius of Toulouse, France, in 405 A.D., giving the same list.

5. **Council of Carthage** in North Africa in 419 A.D.
6. **Council of Nicaea II** in 787 A.D.
7. **Ecumenical Council of Florence** in 1442 A.D.
8. **Council of Trent** formally closed the Canon on April 8th, 1546 A.D.
9. **Catechism of the Catholic Church** in 1992.A.D.

So, the Catholic Church decided what books are inspired, and therefore, teach the truth and are to be in the Bible.

> *I would not believe the Gospel unless moved thereto by the authority of the Church.*
>
> (St. Augustine 354-430 A.D.)

> *We are obligated to yield many things to the Catholics – (for example) that they possess the Word of God which we received from them, otherwise we should have known nothing at all about it.*
>
> (Martin Luther)

How Did the Catholic Church Know Which Books Are Canonical?

The Catholic Church set the standards which a book must pass in order for it to be considered to be inspired and a source of revealed doctrine or canonical.

1. Was it written by an Apostle, or was the authority of an Apostle behind it? Matthew's Gospel was written by the Apostle, Matthew. Mark was not an Apostle but he was the translator for Peter when the latter was in Rome. So, Mark's Gospel had Peter's preaching behind it. Luke's Gospel was rooted in the authority of Paul. John was an Apostle.
2. Was the book used by the Church in its teaching and worship?

3. Did the teaching in the book agree with the teaching of the Catholic Church as handed down by Tradition and the bishops of the Catholic Church?
4. Exotic material was excluded.

The Origin of the New Testament.

Where did the New Testament come from? Who wrote it? When was it written?

The New Testament was written between 50 & 100 A.D. There are 27 books in it. Only 8 or 9 different men wrote those 27 Books. The New Testament consists of these books:

Matthew –	One Gospel
Mark –	One Gospel
Luke –	Two Books – One Gospel and Acts of Apostles
John –	Five Books – One Gospel, Revelation, and Three Epistles
Peter –	Two Epistles or Letters
Jude –	One Epistle
James –	One Epistle
Paul –	Thirteen or Fourteen Epistles.

It is not certain that Paul wrote Hebrews. The New Testament was written in Koine Greek; that is, the Greek that was spoken by the common people in the 1st century.

There are different types of writing in the New Testament; for example, history, parables, apocalyptic texts, etc.

First Thessalonians was the first book of the New Testament to be written. It was written around the year 50 A.D. Paul and the other New Testament writers did not write letters to be put in a book which would be used by Christians for hundreds of years.

Paul wrote letters to:

1. Answer questions about what it meant to be a disciple of Jesus Christ.
2. Solve problems in particular communities.

3. Encourage communities.
4. Remind people about the teachings of Jesus.

These letters were written over a period of about 14 years (50-64) and sent to Christian communities in the Roman Empire. As time went on, they were collected. Pope Clement I (d. 90 A.D.) knew of some of them, Marcion (140 A.D.) quotes from 10 of Paul's letters. We know from a papyrus that Paul's letters had been collected by 200 A.D.

Marcion of Sinope wrote that the God who sent Jesus is a different god than the God of Judaism who created things. He was denounced by the Fathers of the Church, Justin Martyr, Irenaeus, Tertullian and was excommunicated around 144 A.D.

The Gospels were written after Paul died in 64 or 67 A.D.

Who Had the Authority to Put the Bible Together?

Some say that the people put the Bible together.

Others say that very few people could read or write in those days. So, it was the Church that put the Bible together.

What Is The Truth?

Catholic Christians and non-Catholic Christians believe that the Bible is the inspired Word of God. This belief is based on their acceptance of the fact that the Catholic Church had the authority to declare which books were inspired and should be included in the list of sacred books, or "Canon" of the Bible, and which books should not be included.

The Catholic Church knew it had this authority and guidance because Jesus said that He would be with the Church He established and that the Holy Spirit, the Spirit of Truth, would be with His Church.

1. Jesus says in John 14:16-17 that he will ask the Father to send another Paraclete (Counselor) to be with His Church. The Paraclete (Counselor) would be the Spirit of Truth.
2. In John 16:13, Jesus says that this Spirit of Truth will guide His Church to all truth.

3. In Matthew 28:20, Jesus promises to be with His Church always.
4. In Matthew 16:19, Jesus says whatever His Church declares bound or loosed on earth will be bound or loosed in heaven.
5. In Luke 10:16, Jesus tells His Church that "he who hears you, hears Me. He who rejects you rejects Me. And he who rejects Me, rejects Him who sent Me".
6. Paul, in 1Timothy 3:15, calls the Church the pillar and bulwark of the truth.

For more than 1500 years the Catholic Church has accepted and taught that the 73 books of the Bible are inspired and make up the list of sacred books in the Bible. Jesus gave His Apostles and Church the gift of the Holy Spirit when He said. *"Receive the Holy Spirit."* (John 20:22). Jesus also said, *I am with you always until the end of the world."* (Matthew 28:20). This promise was made to the Church alone and not to an individual person.

> *I would not believe the Gospel unless moved thereto by the authority of the Church.*
>
> (St. Augustine)

> *We learn about Christ in the Scriptures; we learn about the Church in the Scriptures. If you accept Christ, why do you not accept the Church.*
>
> (St. Augustine)

How the Bible Was Written

Originally the Bible was written in "uncial" writing. This type of writing consisted of capital letters with no connection between letters, no spaces between words and sentences, no periods or comas and no chapters or verses; for example, GODISNOWHERE. Our modern writing would read: *God is now here,* or God *is nowhere.* So, punctuation, etc., can be very important and translators are aware of that. As in the above example, the meaning can change, depending upon where the spaces and punctuation are placed. Uncial writing was popular from the 4th until the 8th century A.D. Next came "cursive" writing, that is ordinary handwriting with capital letters at the beginning of sentences, letters joined and spaces between words. The earliest cursive manuscript that we have is dated 835 A.D. This kind of writing was popular from the 800's A.D. until the invention of printing in 1450 A.D. From 405 A.D. through 1450 A.D., all Bibles were handwritten by monks in the Catholic monasteries. The materials used were:

1. **Papyrus** (from which we get the name paper) was made from a reed growing on the banks of the Nile River. The reed was cut into strips, glued together and joined into scrolls as long as 35 feet. The pen used was a reed which was cut obliquely across the bottom to form a point. The point was slit so that it would hold and feed ink. The scribe carried a pen knife to keep the point sharp. Since the material easily wore out, the scribe possessed a large number of reeds.
2. Also used were skins of animals:
    a. the skin of sheep or goats, called **parchment**, and
    b. the skin of young calves, called **vellum**. Parchment was of a superior quality compared to papyrus but the latter was more popular for several centuries – possibly because it was less expensive. However, wealthy people preferred the papyrus. Parchment was heavier and did not make a good scroll, which was the usual book form. The inconvenience of the scroll and the difficulty in checking references brought about the end of the scroll. The Codex, which is the modern book form, began to be produced in the 2nd century A.D. It was probably invented by Christians since all the early codices which have been found are almost entirely biblical or Christian. Parchment was bound at the left-hand side. A metal pen or stylus was used to write, and the ink was a combination of soot mixed with gum or glue.

From the 2nd century we find that the monks attached the papyrus sheets or skins together in book form as we do today. This replaced the scrolls. The monks preserved the Bible by copying it repeatedly on newer skins.

In each monastery there was usually one large room, called a **Scriptorium**, or a few smaller rooms, set aside especially for the copying of the Bible. These rooms were built so that they would have all the best possible natural light, thus enabling the monks to work at the task for as many daylight hours as possible. The monks worked in privacy, since copying was such an intense task. Usually, only the monk (scribe) and the superior could enter the scriptorium. Sometimes a group of monks would sit, patiently writing down the text of the Bible as it was read to them by another monk. In this way, several copies would be made at the same time. Lamps, or candles, were seldom used because of the danger of fire. The rooms were not heated so it made the work very difficult in cold weather. When a monk had finished copying one page, he gave it to another monk to check for accuracy. The latter gave it to another monk for decoration, if that was the plan. One of the most beautifully decorated handwritten books done by monks is the Book of Kells. It dates from around 800 A.D., and can be seen at Trinity College, Dublin. It is a manuscript of the Four Gospels.

Many examples of the Bible, or parts of the Bible, can be seen in museums all over the world. The artwork is exquisite with different colors of ink used. These are priceless treasures today. Many covers of the Bibles were made of silver or gold. Precious jewels were also attached to the covers. The Bible was often chained to pulpits so that all people could use them, much like telephone books were attached to telephone booths until recently, but at the same time, one could not easily steal them. At that time all the books in Universities in Europe were chained to tables. Scarcely anyone owned a Bible because it was so expensive and few could read. In the Middle Ages it would take a monk approximately 3 years to copy the Bible in handwriting. The cost would have been about 3 year's wages. For some of the large Bibles it would take the skins of 900 to 1,000 sheep to make up one large Bible – one sheep for each page. So, it was expensive to put a Bible together – 3 years wages, 3 years of a monk's life, and skins of 900 sheep.

The Catholic Church brought to life the stories of the Old and New Testaments for the millions who could not read or write. They did this in the European Cathedrals and Churches through art, including stained glass windows, and sculpture. The art was the Gospel for the poor. Those Cathedrals and Churches are proof that the Catholic Church tried to keep the Bible in the minds of the people. So, even though the people could not read or write, or afford to have a Bible, or be strong enough to carry a Bible (1,000 skins of sheep) they knew the Bible because it was preached to them and shown to them in art form.

Printing was invented by Johann Gutenberg in 1450. Before this, the use of paper was being perfected. This revolutionized the copying of the Bible. Once type was set, accuracy was guaranteed (thus removing the human errors sometimes made by the monks in copying by hand), and the printing was fast. The first book to be printed was the Bible. It is called "The Mazarin Bible" which was printed at Mayence in 1452, at the request of Cardinal Mazarin. By 1522, the Catholic Church had sponsored the printing of 626 editions of the Bible in different languages. Among them were 14 complete editions in High German, 5 complete editions in Low German, 11 Italian editions, 10 French editions, 2 Bohemian editions, 1 Spanish edition, 1 Flemish edition, and 1 Russian edition. Martin Luther translated the New Testament into German in 1522, the Old Testament in 1534, and he put the **Seven Books** between the Old and New Testaments.

The Bible and Martin Luther

Martin Luther indirectly took **Seven Books** out of the Bible. He denied that they had canonical status and, on account of this denial, they eventually disappeared from the Protestant Bible. That is why the Catholic Bible has seven books more than the Protestant Bible.

Jesus, of course, did not give authority to an individual person to decide what books went into the Bible. He gave that authority to the Church which He established.

The Seven Books

What Is The Truth? About The Seven Books?

The Catholic Bible has seven books more in the Old Testament than the Protestant Bible. Did the Catholics add these books? If so, when were they added? What are the names of these books?

Protestants call these books Apocrypha which means hidden. This is not a good name for them. They were never hidden and are not hidden today. In c. 400 A.D. when the Catholic Church compiled the books to be in Scared Scripture (later called the Bible), these **Seven Books** were declared canonical. They have been in the Catholic Bible for nearly 1600 years as of the 21th century. Catholics call these **Seven Books** "Deuterocanonical" which means 'Second Canon'. This also is not a good name. There is no second canon. There is only ONE canon in which all the books and their parts are inspired. These **Seven Books** are just as inspired as the others. The Council of Trent says that they were accepted by the Council Fathers "with equal devotion and reverence."

The **Seven Books** are Judith, Tobit, 1st and 2nd Maccabees, Wisdom, Ecclesiasticus (Sirach) and Baruch. An easy way to remember the names of these books is **J.T. McWEB:** **J**udith, **T**obit, **Mc** 1 & 2 Maccabees, **W** Wisdom, **E** Ecclesiasticus (Sirach), **B** Baruch. Some sections of Esther and Daniel are not considered inspired by Protestants. We will not use the words Deuterocanonical or Apocrypha because those words do not describe those books in a true manner. We will simply call them the **Seven Books**.

These **Seven Books** were NEVER ADDED to the Bible. They were in the Bible for over 1,100 years from 382 to 1545, and then they were demoted and eventually **taken out** by Martin Luther who had absolutely **no** authority to do so. These **Seven Books** were in the *Septuagint* Translation of Jewish Sacred Writings.

Here is a very interesting fact.

All early Protestant English Bible translations contained these **Seven Books:**

The Coverdale Bible – 1535
The Great Bible – 1539
The Geneva Bible – 1560
The King James Bible – 1611

These Bibles had the Seven Books in a section between the Old Testament and the New Testament. The Seven Books are accepted as part of the Bible by the Eastern Orthodox Churches. These Books make up a big part of the Old Testament and bring the history of the chosen people down to c. 134-63 B.C. Nehemiah is the last historical book in the Protestant Bible and only reaches to about 400 B.C.

In his early years, Luther often quoted from some of these **Seven Books**, but later in life he changed his thinking and demoted them.

In 1519, he denied that 2 Maccabees was inspired. In 2 Maccabees, we are told that Judas Maccabeus took up a collection so that sacrifice could be offered for those who had died in battle. 2 Maccabees 12:45-46, says that it is a holy and pious thought to make atonement for the dead that they might be freed from sin. Luther did not agree with praying for the dead. He accepted the Hebrew Old Testament because it agreed with his theology. He said he hated Esther - but that book is in the Protestant Bible. He said a book is canonical if it preached the Gospel as he understood it, but then we do not know what that meant. He rejected any book that did not agree with his theology. In 1545, Luther put the **Seven Books** which he "demoted" into his Bible, but he rearranged the order of them. He put them at the end of the Old Testament. He said they were, "profitable and good to read, but not equal to Holy Scripture."

He rejected some New Testament books also – he gave a lesser status to Hebrews, 2 John, 3 John, James, Jude, 2 Peter and Revelation. However, in the 17th century his followers brought these books back into the New Testament. James 2:14 says that a man is justified by works and not by faith alone. This is the only place in the Bible in which the expression "faith alone" is used. Luther called James, "An epistle of straw." We do not know what he meant by that.

Luther, early in his life, was a strong supporter of private interpretation of scripture. However, later in life, when he saw the disastrous results of people giving opinions supposedly equal to Bible scholars, he changed his opinion.

Did Martin Luther have authority to decide what books should be in the Bible?

Some say he did.

Others say he did not.

What Is The Truth?

The truth is that he did not have the authority to decide what books should be in the Bible. Jesus gave authority to the leaders in the Church which He established, and not to any individual. Luther had no authority to change something which that Church had accepted as true for over 1,100 years to 1545 A.D. We must remember that Jesus said He will be with His Church always unto the end of the world (Matthew 28:20).

John 16:13 says that the Spirit of Truth will guide us to all truth.

Paul said that the Church of the living God is the pillar and ground of the truth. (1Timothy 3:15)

It is inconceivable that Jesus Christ and the Spirit of Truth would lead the Church in a falsehood for 1,100 years before Luther.

Protestants, following Martin Luther, accept the Hebrew Bible which consists of 39 books in the Old Testament. The Jews accept as canonical only books which were written in Hebrew. If Hebrew is a standard for canonicity then the entire New Testament would have to be excluded since it was written in Greek. Luther regarded the Jews as being the only people who could decide what books should go into the Bible. That raises a question – who had the authority to decide what books should go into the New Testament? Luther, himself, did not accept some books which are in the New Testament, but his followers brought them back. Even though he accepted the Hebrew Old Testament he did not respect the theological opinions of the Jews. He claimed that his new canon of the Bible (Hebrew) had no prayers for the dead. However, there is a well-known Jewish tradition of Q'addish where people pray for their dead relative for eleven months after the death.

Luther also ignored all the 1st century Jews who became Christian and who had accepted the Septuagint. He based his decision upon the opinion of non-Christian Jews who rejected, not only the Seven Books in the Septuagint, but also the entire New Testament.

In the catacombs in Rome there are drawings by the early Christians of events which are told in those **Seven Books** rejected by so many, but have been in the Catholic Bible for 1,600 years.

Who Has the Authority to Interpret the Bible?

Some say that any individual can interpret the Bible.

Others say that only the Catholic Church has the authority to interpret the Bible.

What Is The Truth?

Catholics maintain that the authority to interpret the Bible was given by Jesus to His Church and its appointed leaders. The believer who says that he accepts no Church authority in interpretation of Scriptures ends up following another person or makes himself a church unto himself.

In Luke 10:16, Jesus gave his Apostles authority when He said to them that "whoever hears you, hears Me, whoever rejects you rejects Me.", and He said that who "rejects Me, rejects Him Who sent Me." He also said to them, "Whatever you bind on earth will be bound in Heaven. Whatever you loose on earth will be loosed in heaven" (Matthew 16:19).

The Catholic Church has refrained from interpreting individual verses of scripture. The only exceptions are:

1. Matthew 16:17-19 and John 21:15-17 – Jesus appointed Peter as head of the Apostles.
2. James 5:14 – The Sacrament of the Anointing of the Sick
3. Passages about the institution of the Eucharist are to be literally understood.

The Spirit of Truth (John 16:13) may lead the Church to many more truths contained in Scripture.

The Bible in English (before printing)

Various parts of the Bible were translated into Saxon, the language of England at that time, by:

c. 670 Caedmon, a monk
c. 709 Aldhelm, Bishop of Sherborne
c. 735 Venerable Bede, a monk of Jarrow
c. 849-889 King Alfred
c. 955-1020 Aelfric, Archbishop of Canterbury
c. 1020-15th century English, as we know it today, was developed during this time, and translations appeared in the language of the time.
1380 -1382 John Wycliffe produced the first complete translation of the entire Bible in English.

English Translations

The English language has changed over the centuries. Let us look at some examples.

In **1382**, **John Wycliffe** published the first complete English translation of the Bible. Let us see how Matthew 2:16 was written: "Thanne Eroude seynge that he has disseyued of the astomyenes, was full wroth; and he sent and slewe all the children that weren in Bethlehem." The language is scarcely intelligible to us anymore.

In **1611,** the **King James Version** appeared and the verse reads: "Then Herod, when he saw that he was mocked of the wise men, was exceeding wrath, and sent forth and slew all the children that were in Bethlehem...." The language is understandable.

In **1946**, the **Revised Standard Version** says: "Then Herod saw that he had been tricked by the wise men, was in a furious rage, and he sent and killed all the male children in Bethlehem..."

In **1987**, the **New American Bible** translates it: "When Herod realized he had been deceived by the magi, he became furious. He ordered the massacre of all the boys in Bethlehem...."

Printed Bibles - Protestant

1525-1531 Tyndale Bible. Translated by William Tyndale. It was the first English printed version. There were many errors in it (reportedly 30 errors per page), and it was not complete. It was vehement in its attacks on the Catholic Church. The Church, as guardian of the Bible, could not allow the Word of God to be misinterpreted in such a vicious manner, and so the Catholic Church burned Tyndale Bibles. It was the custom of that time to burn the works of opponents, as Luther had done with the books of Canon Law and the letter from Pope Leo. In 1522, John Calvin burned all the copies he could collect of Servetus' Bible at Geneva. Also, King Henry VIII had the Tyndale Bible burned.

1535 Coverdale Bible. This was the first complete English Bible to be printed, and was commissioned by King Henry VIII's Secretary of State, Cromwell.

1537 Matthew's Bible. This was the work of John Rogers and was a mixture of Tyndale's and Coverdale's Bibles.

1539 The Great Bible. This work was supervised by Miles Coverdale. It was the first official Church of England Bible.

1560 Geneva Bible. Sometimes called the Breeches Bible – it said that Adam and Eve made themselves breeches (Genesis 3:7). It was a revision of the Tyndale and Great Bible and was the Bible of Shakespeare, Bunyan and the Puritans. The marginal notes reflected Puritan views.

1568 Bishop's Bible. Replaced the Great Bible of the Church of England.

1611 The King James Version or Authorized Version

King James saw all kinds of Protestant Bibles being published and unusual interpretations given to different passages. So, since he regarded himself as the supreme head of the Church in England, he authorized (hence the name Authorized Version) a new translation to be made, and he appointed fifty-four of the best scholars in England to revise the

Bishop's Bible of 1568. It took them seven years. It was printed in 1611 and was virtually the only Bible used by English-speaking Protestants for over 300 years.

There is a beauty in the language and a majesty of expression in the King James Version. It has had extensive influence on English literature and speech. As the English language changed and as scholarship in ancient languages advanced and archeology made new discoveries, Protestant authorities called for new translations. In the 1800's, Protestant scripture scholars met in St. Louis to work toward a better translation of the King James Version because it had more than 30,000 errors in it. One of these translations is the Revised Standard Version. In the translation of the original King James Version other previous English translations were consulted also, such as the Rheims New Testament (Catholic) which was published 29 years earlier.

The King James Version was originally published with the **Seven Books**, which Luther had denied were canonical, at the end of the Old Testament. Four years later a law was passed which said that if anyone published the King James Version of the Bible without those **Seven Books**, they would be put in prison for one year. However, after 1644 most Protestant Bibles omitted the **Seven Books**. There was also a list of saints in the beginning of this Bible. This shows that the King James Bible owes its origin to the Catholic Church.

1946 Revised Standard Version. The King James translation was again revised.
1970 New English Bible
1973 New International Version
1982 New King James Version
1989 New Revised Standard Version

Printed Bibles - Catholic

1582-1609 Douay-Rheims Version. This translation was done from the *Vulgate* by Gregory Martin and William Allen in Douay and Rheims, France. It was used by English-speaking Catholics for over 350 years.

1749-1763 Challoner Revised Version. Bishop Challoner revised the Douay-Rheims.

1941 Confraternity Revision. It revised only the New Testament.

1944-1951 Knox Bible. Ronald Knox was commissioned by the English Bishops to make a new translation from the *Vulgate*.

1952-1970; 1987 New American Bible. This translation, from the original languages, was commissioned by the American Bishops, and in 1964 was adopted for use in the Liturgy.

1966; 1985 Jerusalem Bible. The Jerusalem Dominicans edited this French translation which was then translated into English.

1965 Revised Standard Version. This Catholic Edition was prepared by a committee of the Catholic Biblical Association of Great Britain. It included wording which reflects Catholic Tradition.

1966 Revised Standard Version. The Old Testament was an updated translation of the King James Version which included the **Seven Books**.

The Catholic Church and the Bible

What Is The Truth? About The Relationship Between The Catholic Church And The Bible?

The Catholic Church Has:

1. Written the New Testament.
2. Decided which books went into The Bible; that is, decided which books are inspired and make up the "Canon" of Scripture.
3. Compiled those books into a collection which it named the "Bible."

4. Preserved the Bible, for the first 1500 years by hand writing each book over and over again on fresh papyrus, or on fresh skins of animals.
5. Preserved the Bible from destruction.
6. Preserved the Bible from error.
7. Defended the Bible through the last 1600 years.
8. Grounded her doctrines upon the Bible.
9. Held the Bible in highest veneration.
10. Interpreted the Bible for all people.
11. Possessed the right to call the Bible Her Book.

These are NOT in the Bible

These are some of the phrases or words that are not in the Bible.

1. "The Lord helps those who help themselves." This was written by Aeschylus, a Greek poet.
2. "Neither a borrower nor a lender be." Written by William Shakespeare in Hamlet.
3. "Cleanliness is next to godliness." Said by John Wesley, founder of Methodism.
4. "The Bible alone is the primary and absolute authority for faith and morals."
5. A list of the inspired books.
6. The word "Trinity", but the teaching is there
7. The word "Purgatory", but the teaching is there
8. The word "Incarnation", but the teaching is there

> I will send you from the Father the Spirit of Truth.
> Jn 15:27

Writings of the New Testament Era & Those Chosen by the Catholic Church to be the "Canon" of the New Testament

Bold - Writings which the Catholic Church decided to be the "Canon" of Scripture of the New Testament.
+ - Writings (existing today) which the Church decided would NOT be included in the "Canon."
* - Writings (no longer in existence) which the Church decided would NOT be included in the "Canon."

GOSPELS	GOSPELS con't	ACTS
*Andrew	**Luke**	*Andrew
*Apelles	*Mary Magdalene	*Apostles (by Leucius)
*Twelve Apostles	*Marcion	*Apostles (by Lentitus)
*Barnabas	**Mark**	*Apostles (by Leontius)
*Bartholomew	**Matthew**	*Apostles (by Leuthon)
*Basilides	*Matthias	**Apostles (by Luke)**
+Birth of Mary	*Merinthus	*Apostles (by the Ebonites)
*Cerinthus	*Nazarenes	*Apostles (by Manichees)
*Egyptians	+Nicodemus	*Apostles (used by Seleucus)
*Ebonites	*Perfection	*John
*Encratites	*Peter	*Paul
*Eve	+Phillip	*Paul and Thecla
*Hebrews	+The Protevangelion	*Peter
*Hesychius	*Scythianus	*Philip
+Infancy of Jesus Christ	*Titan	*Pilate
+Infancy (by Thomas)	*Thaddaeus	*Thomas
John	+Thomas	
*Jude	+Truth	
*Judas Iscariot	*Valentinus	
+Lost Gospel of Peter		

Writings – con't

Bold - Writings which the Catholic Church decided to be the "Canon" of Scripture of the New Testament.
+ - Writings (existing today) which the Church decided would NOT be included in the "Canon."
* - Writings (no longer in existence) which the Church decided would NOT be included in the "Canon."

EPISTLES	EPISTLES con't	EPISTLES con't
+Barnabas	+Ignatius to the Polycarp	**Paul to the Ephesians**
*Christ (to Peter & Paul)	**James**	**Paul to the Philippians**
*Christ (by Manichees)	+Jesus and Abgarus	**Paul to the Colossians**
+Clement to the Corinthians (1)	**John (1)**	**Paul to the Thessalonians (1)**
+Clement to the Corinthians (2)	**John (2)**	**Paul to the Thessalonians (2)**
Hebrews	**John (3)**	**Paul to Timothy (1)**
+Herod and Pilate	**Jude**	**Paul to Timothy (2)**
+Ignatius to the Ephesians	+Paul to the Laodicians	**Paul to Titus**
+Ignatius to the Magnesians	+Paul to the Seneca	**Paul to Philemon**
+Ignatius to the Trallians	**Paul to the Romans**	**Peter (1)**
+Ignatius to the Romans	**Paul to the Corinthians (1)**	**Peter (2)**
+Ignatius to the Philadelphians	**Paul to the Corinthians (2)**	+Polycarp to the Phillippians
+Ignatius to the Smyrnaeans	**Paul to the Galatians**	*Themison (the Montanist)

Writings - con't

Bold - Writings which the Catholic Church decided to be the "Canon" of Scripture of the New Testament.
+ - Writings (existing today) which the Church decided would NOT be included in the "Canon."
* - Writings (no longer in existence) which the Church decided would NOT be included in the "Canon."

REVELATION	OTHER	BOOKS BY
*Cerinthus	+Apostles' Creed	*Andrew
John	+The Didache	*Christ
*Paul	*The Doctrine of Peter	*The Helkesaites
*Peter	*The Judgment of Peter	+Hermas (His Visions 1)
*Philip	*The Preaching of Paul (and Peter)	+Hermas (His Commands 2)
*Stephen	*The Preaching of Peter	+Hermas (His Similitudes 3)
*Thomas	*The Traditions of Matthias	*James
		*John
		*Lentitius
		*Matthew
		*Matthias
		*Paul
		*Thomas

Time-Line of the Number of Books in The Old Testament

CANON OF THE BIBLE is the authentic list of inspired writings that are recognized by the Church and proposed to the faithful as the Word of God and a source of revealed doctrine.

250 B.C. & 100 B.C.	46 Books of Sacred Writings in Septuagint Translation
100 B.C. – 100 A.D.	46 Books accepted as canonical by Jews outside Palestine and many Jews inside Palestine
A.D. – 400 A.D.	46 Books in the Old Testament accepted as canonical by the New Testament Writers and the Early Fathers of the Church and **all Christians**
382 A.D.	46 Books in the Old Testament accepted as canonical by the Council of Rome and by **all Christians**
393 A.D.	46 Books in the Old Testament accepted as canonical by the Council of Hippo and by **all Christians**
397 A.D.	46 Books in the Old Testament accepted as canonical by the Council of Carthage and by **all Christians**
405 A.D.	46 Books in the Old Testament accepted as canonical by Pope Innocent I and by **all Christians**
419 A.D.	46 Books in the Old Testament accepted as canonical by the Council of Carthage and by **all Christians**
787 A.D.	46 Books in the Old Testament accepted as canonical by the Council of Nicaea II and by **all Christians**
1442 A.D.	46 Books in the Old Testament accepted as canonical by the Council of Florence and by **all Christians**
1534 A.D.	**Seven Books** stolen from Old Testament By influence of Martin Luther Leaving those who broke away from the Church only **39 Books** Thus, introducing **the Protestant Bible**.
1546 A.D.	46 Books in the Old Testament accepted as canonical by The Council of Trent (CANON FORMALLY CLOSED)
1992 A.D.	46 Books accepted as canonical by The Catechism of the Catholic Church

Part Three – Frequently Asked Questions

Truth is truth,
No matter how many people refuse to believe it.
And
A lie is a lie,
No matter how many people embrace it.

(Archbishop Fulton Sheen)

Truth Never goes away.
Christ is Truth.
God Professes Truth to Us.

Throughout history there have been many people who claimed that they were messengers from God.

How can we know if a person's claim is true or not?

A true messenger from God will be able to prove his or her authenticity by miracles and prophecy.

A MIRACLE is an out of the ordinary event or feat that can only be explained by the direct intervention of God. Only God can work miracles.

A PROPHECY is the foretelling of future events which depend on the free will of God or people, and these events could not be guessed at. Only God can know them.

Whenever there is an important event coming up there are announcements concerning the event. If a wedding is being planned, invitations are sent out announcing the upcoming event. The same is true with God. God promised that a big event would take place, and that event would be the coming of a Messiah or Anointed One. God made preparations for this coming event. He sent prophets or messengers to announce to the people of Israel to prepare for this coming event.

In the Old Testament, the prophets, or messengers from God, foretold several things about the coming of the Messiah – that He would be born of a virgin in Bethlehem, and many other things about His life, suffering and death, and that He would perform miracles.

All these miracles and prophecies were fulfilled in one man. This man has made the greatest impact on the most people throughout the past 2,000 years. That man is Jesus Christ.

Jesus worked miracles by healing the sick, raising the dead, having power over nature and the devils. These miracles were performed in the open and could be seen even by His enemies. His greatest miracle was rising from the dead – which He foretold.

Jesus made many prophecies. He foretold that Judas would betray Him, that Peter would deny Him, that the Apostles would run away, that He would suffer and die and rise from the dead and ascend into heaven. He foretold the destruction of Jerusalem and so on. All of His prophecies came true.

Jesus claimed that He was from God, and, in fact, He claimed He is God. His miracles and prophecies prove that His claim is the truth.

Many have claimed that they were messengers from God. The questions would have to be:

1. Was their coming and events in their lives foretold?
2. Did God work miracles through them? Only God can work miracles and if God worked miracles through those who claimed to be messengers from Him then that would indicate their claim was the truth.
3. Did they prophecy or tell of events which came true? If so, then that would indicate that their claim was the truth.

I Am the Way, the Truth and the Life. Jn 14:6

Was Latin forced upon people?

Some say that Latin was forced on the people by Pope Gregory I about 600 A.D.

Others say that Latin was the language which the people spoke, and that is why the Church used it in prayer and worship.

What Is The Truth?

The Catholic Church utilized Aramaic (the language spoken by Jesus) first; then Greek (the language of the people at that time); and then, in the late 4th century, Latin became the language of the people and thus became the language used by the Catholic Church for several hundred years.

Were Bells Baptized?

Some say bells were baptized on the instruction of Pope John XIII about 965 A.D.

Others say bells were blessed.

What Is The Truth?

Catholics baptized people, not bells. If they baptized bells then they could baptize books, vestments, computers, etc. Whenever a church received bells, then those bells were blessed, not baptized. Any person, place or thing can be blessed or dedicated for a sacred purpose.

Transubstantiation

Some say Transubstantiation was invented by Pope Innocent III in 1215 A.D.

Others say Transubstantiation was always in the Church.

What Is The Truth?

Transubstantiation means that bread and wine are changed into the Body, Blood, Soul and Divinity of Jesus Christ at Mass. This belief was in the Catholic Church from the time of the Apostles, but theologians could never come up with a word that described this belief. In 1215, the 4th Lateran Council used this term to describe what happens at Mass. The belief comes from John's Gospel, Chapter 6, from 1 Corinthians Chapter 11, and from the description of the Last Supper in the Gospels. So, the belief was in the Catholic Church from the time of the Apostles and the word "Transubstantiation" was chosen by the 4th Lateran Council in 1215 – to state this truth.

Forbidden Books

Some say the Bible was placed on the list of Forbidden Books by the Council of Valencia in 1229 A.D.

Others say that in 1557 Pope Paul IV established the "Index of Prohibited Books". It was a list of books that Catholics were prohibited from reading.

What Is The Truth?

1. There was no council held in Valencia, Spain, in 1229.
2. In 1229, the Muslims were in control of Valencia and would not have allowed Catholic bishops to meet in one of their cities.
3. A list of the Forbidden Books was not set up until 1557, 328 years AFTER the Bible supposedly was on the list. The list of 1557 was called "Index of Prohibited Books".
4. There was a Council held in 1229 in Toulouse, France, to deal with the Albigensian Heresy. The Albigensians had published a Bible which was not translated accurately and which supported their false claims. The bishops, at the Council of Toulouse, forbade the reading of this Bible to protect the people from false teachings. The bishops were simply doing what they were supposed to do – protect and hand on the truth as revealed by Jesus Christ to His Apostles, and the Apostles handed it on to their successors; that is, the bishops in the Catholic Church.

Was Peter Called the Pope?

What Is The Truth?

Peter never claimed to be the Pope. The title was not conferred on the bishops of Rome during the earlier years of the Church. In the same way we can say that the Bible did not claim to be "the Bible" in the earlier years because that term had not been thought of until many years later.

Was Peter Ever in Rome?

The Bible does not say explicitly that he was there, but 1 Peter 5:13 does imply that he was. Tertullian (c. 160-220), and some other early Christian writers, say that Peter went to Rome, was in charge of the Church there and was martyred during the persecution of Nero in 67 A.D.

None of the early writers claim that Peter never went to Rome. No other city claimed to be the place where Peter died or was buried.

In excavations in Rome, which took place between 1939-1968, the bones of Peter were found. After research, this was confirmed by Pope Paul VI.

Mary – Honor to Her

Some say that Mary, the Mother of Jesus, is being worshiped by Catholics.

Others say that Mary should be treated like any other woman.

What Is The Truth?

Do Catholics really worship Mary?
NO. Worship is for God alone. Catholics do NOT worship Mary.

Do Catholics honor Mary?
Yes. So do Orthodox, many Anglicans and many Lutherans. Martin Luther was very emphatic that honor should be given to Mary. Martin Luther, himself, had a strong devotion to her.

Why honor Mary?
These are some of the reasons:
The Holy Trinity (Father, Son and Holy Spirit) honored her.

1. God the Father honored her. The Father sent the angel Gabriel to ask her if she would become the Mother of Jesus, the Son of God. The angel said to her that she had found favor with God. (Luke 1:28-38)

   This is a very high compliment from the Father. The Father honored her by asking her to be the mother of His Son.

2. God the Son honored her.
   a. Jesus lived in her for nine months.
   b. Mary gave birth to Jesus. (Luke 2:7)
   c. Jesus went down with Mary and Joseph and came to Nazareth, and was subject to them. (Luke 2:51)
   d. Like any good Jew, Jesus obeyed the Commandments, including the Fourth Commandment. "Honor your father and your mother..." (Exodus 20:12)
3. The Holy Spirit honored her. The angel Gabriel told Mary that the Holy Spirit would come upon her, and she would have a son. (Luke 1:35)
4. Mary was present at the beginning of Jesus' public ministry, and influenced Him to perform His first miracle. They ran out of wine at the wedding at Cana in Galilee. Mary told Jesus what was happening. Then, Jesus changed the water into wine. (John 2:3-11)
5. Mary was present at the end of Jesus' public ministry. She was at the foot of the cross on Calvary. Jesus saw His mother, and the disciple whom He loved standing by. (John 19:26)
6. Mary was with the disciples in the upper room as they prepared and awaited the coming of the Holy Spirit. (Acts 1:14)
7. Mary is honored because she was Blessed Among Women as the angel Gabriel told her. (Luke 1:28)
8. Mary is looked upon as a model for all followers of her Son. Mary said "Yes" to the Will of the Father. She accepted to be the Mother of the Son of God. (Luke 1:38) Consequently, Mary was the first to accept Jesus Christ. She was the first Christian.
9. Mary, like all good followers of her Son, always brings people to Him. Mary tells us, as she told the servants at the wedding in Cana in John 2:5 to do whatever He tells us.
10. Those who honor Mary seek her intercession with God on their behalf. The role of her intercession is foreshadowed in the Old Testament. The kings had many wives. So, on account of her close relationship to the king, the mother of the king was the queen of the kingdom. This made her the most powerful representative of the people to the king. Bathsheba, the mother of

King Solomon, went to him to speak to him for Adonijah. The king rose up to meet her and bowed down to her, and sat down on his throne and had a throne set for her; so, she sat at his right hand. He told her to ask for whatever she wanted, and he would not refuse her. (1 Kings 2:19-20)

11. Lastly, to honor Mary fulfills Scripture itself. Mary said that all generations would call her blessed (Luke 1:48). That is why Mary is referred to as The Blessed Virgin Mary.

Mary - Always A Virgin

Some say that Mary had other children besides Jesus.

Others say that Mary was a virgin before and after Jesus was born.

Some people read in the Bible "brethren of the Lord" and presume that Mary had children other than Jesus.

What Is The Truth?

What Does the Bible Say?

A document, written around 120 A.D. called the "Protoevangelium of James" is in existence. It sets out to prove that Mary was a virgin, both before and after Jesus was born. There would have been people alive then who knew Mary. Nobody disputed the claim that Mary, the mother of Jesus, was always a virgin.

"Brethren" can mean different relationships.

It can mean:

1. Sons of the same parent. Rebekah told Jacob, her son, that she heard his father speak to Esau, his brother. (Genesis 27:6)
2. Nephew. Lot was the nephew of Abraham (Genesis 11:27), and yet Abraham calls Lot his brethren or kinsman. (Genesis 13:8) Some translations use kinsman. The Hebrew word is "ahim" which translates literally to brother but can be used for male relatives or kinsman.
3. Friend. David calls Jonathan his brother while Jonathan is, in fact, his friend. (2 Samuel 1:26)

4. Members of the same race or nation. "If your brother, a Hebrew man, or a Hebrew woman ..." (Deuteronomy 15:12)
5. Members of a related nation. God said not to hate an Edomite, for he is your brother. (Deuteronomy 23:7)
6. Stephen, in his address to the council, uses the word brethren many times. (Acts 7:2-53)

Those who revolted against the Church – Martin Luther, John Calvin & Ulrich Zwingli – believed that Mary was always a virgin and acknowledged it as the teaching of the Bible.

In the New Testament, Christians are called brothers about 160 times. Jesus Himself says that a person who does the Will of the Father is His own brother.

Some New Testament examples:

"By Silvanus, our faithful brother as I consider him..."

(1 Peter 5:12)

"I, John, both your brother and companion ..."

(Revelation 1:9)

The brethren of the Lord were not other children of Mary because:

1. The Bible does not say that Mary had other children.
2. If Mary had other children, why would Jesus, when he was dying on the cross, have given His mother into the care of John the Apostle? (John 19:26-27)
3. In Hebrew and Aramaic, there is no word for "cousin." Aramaic is the language spoken by Jesus. To mean "cousin" they would have to talk around it, so they chose to use the term "brother."
4. "(Joseph) did not know her till she had brought forth her first-born Son (Matthew 1:25)." This seems to imply that Joseph and Mary lived together as husband and wife and had other children

after her firstborn Son was born. "Till," meaning "until" had a different meaning when the Bible was written than it has today. When the Bible was written "till" meant that an event did not happen up to a certain point in time. It did not imply that it happened after that point in time. Firstborn does not mean that others were born afterwards. To the ancient Jews, it meant whatever opened the womb.

Similarly, 2 Samuel 6:23 says that Michal, the daughter of Saul, had no children to the day of her death. "To" is often translated "till" or "until", and of course, does not imply that she had children after her death.

So, the Truth is: Mary was a virgin before and after she gave birth to Jesus.

Was Jesus An Only child?

What Is The Truth?

Yes, in the biological sense. In the spiritual sense, He has millions of brothers and sisters, if they do the Will of the Father.

From the early Church there are other writers who say that Mary was always a virgin.

Ignatius of Antioch (d. 110)
Irenaeus (c. 130-202)
Hilary of Poitiers (354 A.D.)
Jerome (383 A.D.)
Pope Siricius I (392 A.D.)
Pope Leo I (450 A.D.)
Justin Martyr (100-165)
Origen (248 A.D.)
Athanasius (360 A.D.)
Ambrose of Milan (388 A.D.)
Augustine (401 A.D.)

Protestants, as a whole, accept the teachings of early Councils of the Church. Three of the seven Ecumenical Councils of the Church clearly and emphatically teach that Mary was always a virgin. They are Constantinople II (553 A.D.). Constantinople III (680 A.D.), and Nicaea II (787 A.D.)

The Bible NEVER speaks of the "Children of Mary". It does speak of "Mary, Mother of Jesus", but never "Mary, Mother of Jesus, James, Joseph, and daughters".

Mark 6:3 says, "Is he not the son of Mary.", not "a" son of Mary.

In the Old and New Testament, the term brother could mean different relationships.

So, the Truth is: Jesus was her only child.

Statues

Some say that Catholics worship statues.

Others say that Catholics do not worship statues.

What Is The Truth?

Catholics do NOT worship statues.

A statue is simply a piece of marble or a chuck of plaster. Statues, paintings, or icons are used to recall to one's mind the person depicted. It is easier to remember one's mother or father by looking at their photograph. It is easier to recall the lives of the saints by looking at statues, icons, paintings or photographs of them.

Statues were used in the Old Testament. God instructed Moses to make cherubim of gold for the top of the Ark of the Covenant in Exodus 25:18-20. Also in Numbers 21:8-9 God told Moses to make a fiery serpent and set it on a pole. Everyone who had been bitten by a serpent and looked upon that bronze serpent would live. All Christians use picture books to teach about Jesus Christ. These pictures are a kind of statue.

Americans could not be accused of worshiping statues of the Statue of Liberty, Abraham Lincoln or the many statues in every State of the Nation.

Infant Baptism

Some say that children should be baptized after they are born.

Others say that they should not be baptized and that they should be free to make their own commitment to Jesus Christ when they become adults.

What Is The Truth?

Jesus said, "Let the children come to me ..." (Mt 19:14) (Luke 18:16).

Since Jesus said this, who are we to prevent children from coming to Him in baptism?

Paul teaches that baptism has replaced circumcision (Col 2:11-12). Usually only infants were circumcised under the Old Law. Paul talks about baptism as "the circumcision of Christ" which is the equivalent of circumcision.

If it were the custom of the early Church to baptize children only after they reached the use of reason then it would have been explicitly stated in the Bible. There is no reference to this in the Bible. So, infants were baptized in the early Church.

In Acts 16:15, we are told that Lydia was converted by Paul's preaching and that she was baptized, with her household. Paul and Silas had converted the Philippian jailer to the faith, and he was baptized, with all his family (Acts 16:33). So, whole households were baptized. That would include children.

Origen (244 A.D.) said that baptism was given to infants.

The Council of Carthage (253 A.D.) condemned the opinion that baptism should be withheld from infants until the 8th day after birth.

St. Augustine (408 A.D.) said that baptizing infants goes back to the time of the Apostles.

In the early Church, faith in the Lord was necessary for an adult convert to receive baptism, but it was not necessary for the children of believers. Nowhere in the Bible does it say that Baptism is for adults only, and that children should not be baptized.

If one says that a child should not be baptized, then that gives rise to other questions. Parents make all the decisions for their child in the child's early life. They make sure that all the physical, intellectual and emotional needs of the child are met. Decisions are made about doctor's and dentist's visits, information for attendance at schools and universities and ensuring that the child realizes he/she is loved. When the child becomes an adult, he or she makes their own decisions about all those things and also about spiritual matters. Why should the spiritual life of the child be ignored and treated as being unimportant when, in actual fact, it is the most important issue as it concerns eternal life.

Purgatory

Some say that there are only 2 places where we can go after death, and these places are Heaven and Hell.

Others say that there is a third place where we can go – a place or condition where we are cleansed of lesser sins in order to be free from all sin and get into heaven. This place is called "Purgatory".

What Is The Truth?

The Catechism of the Catholic Church states in these paragraphs:

1030 All who die in God's grace and friendship, but still imperfectly purified, are indeed assured of their eternal salvation; but after death they undergo purification, so as to achieve the holiness necessary to enter the joy of heaven.

1031 The Church gives the name Purgatory to this final purification of the elect, which is entirely different from the punishment of the damned. The Church formulated her doctrine of faith on Purgatory especially at the Councils of Florence and Trent. The tradition of the Church, by reference to certain texts of Scripture, speaks of a cleansing fire: As for certain lesser faults, we must believe that, before the Final Judgment, there is a purifying fire. He who is truth says that whoever utters blasphemy against the Holy Spirit will be pardoned neither in this age nor in the age to come. From this sentence we understand that certain offenses can be forgiven in this age, but certain others in the age to come.

1032 This teaching is also based on the practice of prayer for the dead, already mentioned in Sacred Scripture: "Therefore [Judas Maccabeus] made atonement for the dead, that they might be delivered from their sin." From the beginning the Church has honored the memory of the dead and offered prayers in suffrage for them, above all the Eucharistic sacrifice, so that, thus purified, they may attain the beatific vision of God. The Church also commends almsgiving, indulgences, and works of penance undertaken on behalf of the dead: Let us help and commemorate them. If Job's sons were purified by their father's sacrifice, why would we doubt that our offerings for the dead bring them some consolation? Let us not hesitate to help those who have died and to offer our prayers for them.

The Council of Florence (1439) and the Council of Trent (1563) taught the same doctrine on Purgatory.

The Church has made no official statement on the nature and intensity of suffering in Purgatory. What must be believed as "of faith" by Catholics is that there is a Purgatory, and that souls detained in it are helped by the prayers of the faithful (Creed of St. Pius V). That there is FIRE in Purgatory has never been defined by the Church.

The writings of the Fathers of the Church and council decrees point out that this is an ancient and universal belief, and no serious scholar has ever denied it. All the ancient Mass liturgies provide prayers not only for the living, but also for the dead. Vatican I and II stress prayers for the dead.

The early Church insisted on prayers for the dead based on scriptural grounds. These are some of the early writers who insisted on prayers for the dead.

Justin Martyr	100-165 A.D.
Irenaeus of Lyons	130-202 A.D.
Tertullian	c. 160-220 A.D.
Origen	185-254 A.D.
Cyprian of Carthage	c. 200-258 A.D.
Cyril of Jerusalem	313-386 A.D.
Eusebius of Caesarea	265-339 A.D.
Epiphanius	310-403 A.D.
Ambrose	340-397 A.D.
Jerome	342-420 A.D.
John Chrysostom	347-407 A.D.
Augustine	354-430 A.D.

ALL uphold the traditional Catholic doctrine on praying for the dead.

The word Purgatory is not mentioned in the Bible. Neither is Trinity, Sunday Observance, Bible, Altar Call, Books of the Gospels, Books of the New Testament, Incarnation, etc.

The words Trinity and Incarnation are not found in the Bible, yet these doctrines are clearly taught there, and these are teachings which every Christian must believe.

Bible texts which the Church says applies to Purgatory are 2 Maccabees 12:44-46.

The Second Book of Maccabees is true history. The book accurately reflects the religious beliefs of the Jews at that time. A little more than 100 B.C. the Jews prayed for their dead and still do today. If praying for the dead were wrong, then Jesus would have condemned it. He did not.

In Matthew's Gospel 12:32, Jesus said that anyone who speaks a word against the Son of Man will be forgiven; but whoever speaks against the Holy Spirit, it will not be forgiven, either in this age or in the age to come. This means that sin can be forgiven in the age to come – after death. If someone is in Hell, then they will not want their sins forgiven. If someone is in Heaven, then they have no sins. So, there must be another place where sins can be forgiven.

Luke 12:59, a person will not be freed until the last penny has been paid.

The only person in ancient times known by name to have objected to praying for the dead was Arius, a 4th century priest who left the Church and started his own church.

Praying for the dead presumes an intermediate state of purification, whatever one may call it. Catholics call it Purgatory.

Tertullian (c. 160-220) wrote, "The faithful widow... offers prayers on the anniversary of her husband's death".

During the first 1500 years of the Church, there was no doubt about the necessity of praying for the dead. Those prayers would help souls in Purgatory to get to heaven more speedily. Martin Luther and some others talked against praying for the dead, and that is the reason why Protestants today do not pray for their deceased relatives and friends. The custom of praying for the dead is more than 2000 years old and goes back before the time of Jesus. The custom of not praying for the dead is less than 500 years old.

Revelation 21:27 says that nothing that profanes shall enter Heaven. Then, a person who dies with a very small sin on their soul would be doomed to Hell for all eternity. But God is merciful. He gave us a place or state where we are purified before we enter heaven, and that place or state is called Purgatory. Purgatory is not a sign of God's anger. It is a wonderful example of God's infinite mercy. **It is NOT a second chance. Our final destination is determined by the condition of our soul at the moment of our death**; that is, heaven, for all eternity; hell, for all eternity; or Purgatory, until our soul is cleansed of all venial sins, and then, we go to heaven.

Confession

Some say there is no need to confess our sins to a priest.

Others say that Jesus gave this gift of forgiving sins to His Church.

What Is The Truth?

Read John 20:19-23. On Easter Sunday, the day Jesus rose from the dead, He gave His Apostles the power to forgive sins. There is a connection between the Resurrection of Jesus from the dead and the raising of a soul from the death of sin. Jesus gave this power by breathing on the Apostles. There is another place in the Bible when God breathed on someone (Genesis 2:7). He breathed life into the first human being.

Jesus gives the Apostles the authority to forgive or not to forgive sin. How can a priest know when not to forgive sins? When he hears what the sins are, then he knows whether to forgive or not to forgive the sins.

Some people say, "I confess my sins only to God and Catholics confess their sins only to priests." This is not true. Catholics always confess their sins to God. They do it directly as well as indirectly through the priest because that is what Jesus Christ requires. This is clearly in the Bible. See John 20:19-23.

Many Christians believe that sins are wiped away in Baptism. This means they believe that their ministers are used by God as His instruments in the forgiveness of sins through a Sacrament, Baptism, which they administer.

Catholics believe that God uses the priest as His instrument for the forgiveness of sins in three Sacraments: Baptism, Confession, and Anointing of the Sick.

All believe that God can use their ministers as instruments for physical healing. God can do the same with spiritual healing, if He wishes. Spiritual healing is more important than physical healing.

In the Sacrament of Confession Jesus gives us many important gifts:

1. The certainty of forgiveness of sins
2. Humility
3. Spiritual Direction
4. Help to overcome our justifications for our sins

Christ gave His Apostles the power to forgive sins. He intended that this power to be passed on because He knew that people would sin right up to the end of the world. The early Christians believed this power WAS passed on to the Apostles' successors.

The early Church practiced Confessions.

1. Didache (c.50-150 A.D.) "having confessed your transgressions."
2. Letter of Barnabas (c.75 A.D.) "you shall confess your sins."
3. Ignatius of Antioch (c.110 A.D.) "... the exercises of repentance."
4. St Irenaeus of Lyons (c. 189 A.D.) "make a public confession of their sins."
5. Origen of Alexandria (c. 249 A.D.) "when the sinner does not shrink from declaring his sin to a priest of the Lord..."

Jesus had the authority to forgive sins and gave the authority to the Apostles.

1. Mt 9:2-8, Jesus has authority on earth to forgive sins.
2. Mk 6:7, Jesus sent out the Twelve, two by two and gave them authority over unclean spirits. Jesus gave them His authority.
3. 2 Cor 5:17-20, Paul says the Lord has given the Apostles the ministry of reconciliation. That's how the Apostles did it.

Jesus gave His Apostles the power to forgive sins, but He did not tell them how to use that power. He left that to be decided by His Church.

The Bible Alone (Sola Scriptura)

Some say Sola Sciptura or the Bible Alone is the primary and absolute authority, the final court of appeal for all doctrine and practice (faith and morals) and that

The Bible –
nothing more,
nothing less,
and nothing else –
is all that is necessary for faith and practice.

Others say that the Bible, Tradition and the Teaching Authority of the Church (Magisterium; that is, the Pope and all the bishops united with him) are needed to fully discern God's Revelation.

What Is The Truth?

If the Bible and nothing else is all that is necessary for faith and practice, then the Bible itself should make this doctrine clear, or at least imply this doctrine.

But
the Bible does NOT say
the Bible does NOT imply
that it alone is all that is necessary for faith and practice.

The Bible does NOT claim that God can hand down revelation only in written form.

The Bible and two other sources are needed to fully discern God's revelation: Sacred Tradition and the teaching office of the Church (Magisterium) are also necessary. Around the year 40 A.D. a problem arose in the Church – circumcision. The Jewish Scripture emphatically said that Gentiles should be circumcised. God Himself had commanded this in Gen. 17 and Ex. 12:48. Jesus did not do away with this.

In 50 A.D., the Church held a council, the Council of Jerusalem, so that the Magisterium of the Church (Apostles) could examine Scripture, Tradition (written & unwritten) and then make a decision.

The decision was that circumcision was not necessary in order for the Gentiles to become Christians.

The Council handled the problem as the Catholic Church handles problems today – like a three-legged stool:

1. written Tradition (Bible)
2. unwritten Tradition
3. Magisterium

That is the reason why St. Paul tells the Thessalonians (2 Thes 2:15) to hold fast to the traditions which they were taught by him and others, either by word of mouth or by letter.

Sola Scriptura does not work in practice. That is why there are almost 34,000 different Christian denominations today – all saying they are adhering to Sola Scriptura, or the Bible alone.

Catholics accept the Bible as an authority in matters of faith because it is God's inspired Word (The Catholic Church tells us that the Bible is the inspired Word of God.) But we cannot accept that the Bible is the ONLY rule of faith for the following reasons.

1. The Bible itself does NOT teach that. The Bible itself does NOT teach that Sola Scriptura (The Bible Alone) is the only authority in the matters of faith. The Bible actually tells us that we need MORE than just the Bible. John 21:25 says that not everything Jesus said and did is recorded in scripture. The Bible also says that we must hold fast to oral tradition, the preached Word of God (1 Cor. 11:2; 1 Pet 1:25). 2 Pet 3:15-16 tells us that sacred scripture can be very difficult to interpret. This means that we need an interpreter who has authority. 1 Tim 3:15 says that the

Church is "the pillar and foundation of truth." It does not say that the Bible is the pillar and foundation of truth.

2. The doctrine "The Bible Alone" goes against history. The Catholic Church was the authority which put the Bible together. The Church decided what was inspired and should be included in the Canon of the Bible. (1 Tim 3:15)
3. The doctrine of "The Bible Alone" goes against common sense. If a document is meant to play a vital role in deciding how people live, then there must be a living, continuing authority to interpret it, and to guard it. If everyone can interpret the document on their own, then there is chaos. The Founding Fathers of the United States put the Constitution together. But they knew there would be chaos if they did not set up a living, continuing authority to interpret and guard it. That is the Supreme Court. The Founding Fathers were wise, but God is much wiser.

The Church, with the authority to decide what is the infallible Word of God, must have the infallible authority and guidance of the Holy Spirit. Apart from the declarations of the Catholic Church, we have no guarantee that what is in the Bible is the genuine Word of God. To trust the Bible is to trust the authority of the Catholic Church which guarantees the Bible. It is a contradiction to accept the Bible and reject the authority of the Catholic Church.

So, people who quote the Bible as authoritative have no way of determining which books are inspired – unless they accept the teaching authority of the Catholic Church.

If the Bible alone is the primary and absolute authority for faith and morals, then what did the early Christians do since they had no Bible for almost 400 years, and what about those thousands of people who:

1. could not read or write, or
2. could not get a Bible since Bibles were so scarce and so expensive?

Jesus sent the Holy Spirit at Pentecost around 33 A.D. The New Testament was written between 50 and 100 A.D. So, for 20 years there were NO writings which the people could follow, and it was almost another 350 years until a list of the inspired books of the New Testament was approved. How was the message of Jesus transmitted to the people? It was done by Tradition, or word of mouth. The Apostles were told to "Go, teach" not "Go, write." As a matter of fact, only 5 of the 12 Apostles wrote something.

None of the Fathers ever taught Sola Scriptura before the Reformation. It is a teaching of men. This teaching did not come about in the Church for over 1,500 years. It only raised its head in the Protestant Revolt.

> *I would not believe the Gospel unless moved thereto by the Authority of the Church.*
>
> (St. Augustine 354 - 430 A.D.)

Is the Pope the Antichrist?

Some say that the Pope is the Head of the Catholic Church.

Others say that the Pope is the Antichrist.

What Is The Truth?

This statement reflects poorly, not on the Pope, but on Christ. It implies that the Pope is more powerful than Christ, which is absurd.

There have been 266 Popes, and there is a Pope now. In the first 300 years, of the first 31 popes, 28 died violent deaths as martyrs and all were declared saints. If the Pope is the Antichrist, why has Christ not done away with him or especially with the office? He has had almost 2,000 years to do it.

The Bible and the Catholic Church.

Some say that the Catholic Church does not teach what the Bible teaches.

Others say that the Catholic Church put the Bible together and that the teaching in the Bible and the Catholic Church are the same.

What Is The Truth?

The Bible is important because it is God's Word. God speaks to His people in many ways – prayer, through nature and world events, and in daily life and relationships. The Church which Jesus established is commissioned to be the interpreter of His Word to the world. The Church will never teach anything contrary to the Bible. The believer who claims that he/she accepts no Church authority in interpreting the Bible often ends up following a particular preacher or group, or believing just what he/she wants to believe and not necessarily the truth.

Martin Luther said that every person should interpret the Bible according to his own mind. However, he rejected that later in life when he saw people claiming to interpret the Bible as good as any Bible scholar.

> There is a duty upon everyone to search for the truth.

Has the Catholic Church changed its Doctrines?

We must clear up something: the difference between Doctrine and Discipline.

- A Doctrine is an unchangeable truth revealed by God; for example, the Virgin birth.
- A Discipline is a changeable regulation; for example, the Mass in the vernacular (language of the people) instead of in Latin.

The Catholic Church teaches that there can be no new doctrine since the death of the last Apostle. Doctrines can develop; that is, they can be more fully understood and explained in a better way. This understanding is passed on by the Church through its teaching office which is called the Magisterium.

Has the Catholic Church changed its teachings over the centuries?

The Catholic Church has suffered at the hands of emperors, kings, queens and all kinds of regimes, but it has not only survived all of them but has preserved the truths revealed by Jesus 2,000 years ago. The truths proclaimed by the Catholic Church in the early centuries are the very same truths proclaimed by the Catholic Church today.

> Truth never changes.

Joining Another Christian Church

Some say that it is O.K. to join any church, and that there is only one God and that one church is as good as another.

Others say that the Son of God, Jesus Christ, established only one Church, and He is calling everyone to become a member of that Church since it has the full truth which He revealed.

There is a duty upon everyone to search for the truth.

What Is The Truth?

The Bible and Church history clearly tell us that Christ established only ONE Church. However, today we have nearly 34,000 Christian denominations. If a person joins one of the other churches, does it really matter?

It certainly DOES matter. If Christ founded only ONE Church, then all other Christian churches were founded by men.

The members of these churches believe a great deal that is true (they have the Bible), and they are sincere followers of Christ, yet why should a person choose a church that was founded by man instead of the Church that was founded by Christ and which has taught the unchangeable truth for almost 2,000 years?

Are We Roman Catholic?

Some say that the Church is Roman Catholic.

Others say that the Church is the Catholic Church.

What Is The Truth?

The earliest record we have of the terms "Roman Catholic" comes from a report to Queen Elizabeth I from a British secret agent in Rome who referred to "Romish Catholiques" in England and Ireland. This was in the 1500's.

In 107 A.D., Ignatius of Antioch first used the terms "Catholic Church" while he was being brought to Rome to be martyred. He did not use the term "Roman Catholic Church."

Ignatius wrote of a VISIBLE, not an INVISIBLE, Universal Church. This was in 107 A.D. There was and is, only ONE Catholic Church.

The Eastern Orthodox Churches went a separate way in 1054, and the Church of England separated in the 16th century.

The Pope has nine titles but not one of these titles says that he is the Head of a "Roman Catholic Church".

The Catholic Church was not "Roman Catholic" after it was founded by Jesus Christ, so why should it change its name to be "Roman Catholic" today?

If someone says that they are "Roman Catholic", it can mean that they are just one of the many "Catholic" Churches, and all of them, or nearly all of them, claiming to be legitimate. There are, for example,

The Anglo-Catholic Church
The Old Catholic Church
The Polish National Catholic Church
The Greek Catholics
The Byzantine Catholics
And the list goes on.
Some are in union with Rome.

There was only ONE Catholic (Universal) Church for over 1,000 years. Then there was a schism (this is a Greek word meaning "to tear"). The Orthodox Churches separated from the authority of the Pope.

The Catholic Church is "Roman" in the sense that:

1. The head of the Church is in Rome – the Pope.
2. It uses Latin.
3. It uses the Western Rite whereas the Orthodox Churches use the Eastern Rite.
4. The location of the "head office" is in Rome.

To sum up, the Catholic Church is simply "Catholic" (Universal) as it has been called for almost 2,000 years.

Calling Priests Father

Some say that Catholics call the priest "father?" Is that not against Scripture?

Others say priests are called father because when they administer the Sacraments of Baptism, Confession and Anointing of the Sick, they give life to the soul.

Jesus, in Matthew 23:9-10, tells us to call no one on earth our father and that we have but one Father in heaven. He also says that we are not to be called Master; we have but one master, the Messiah.

Jesus is saying that there is only one Father, One Creator, and all fatherhood comes from Him. Paul says in Ephesians 3:14-15 that he kneels before the Father, from whom every family in heaven and on earth is named.

We are all members of God's family. We call Him "Our Father".

<u>What does Paul say about this?</u>

> Paul says that they who preached the Gospel to the Thessalonians treated each one of them as a father treats his children. (1 Thessalonians 2:11)
> Paul, in 1 Corinthians 4:14-17, calls the people his beloved children. He also said that he became their father in Christ Jesus. He calls Timothy his beloved and faithful son. See also 2 Tim 1:2 and 2:1.
> In 1 Timothy 1:2, Paul calls Timothy his true child in faith.
> In Titus 1:4, Paul calls Titus his true child, and in Philemon 1:10, he calls Onesimus his child.

In the above passages, Paul considers himself a spiritual father. The priest is a spiritual father in the same way – he gives spiritual life to his people; that is, when he baptizes them, forgives their sins, preaches the Gospel to them, etc.

If we take Jesus' statement exactly as it is, "Do not call anyone on earth your father", then we cannot call our biological father by the name of father either. On an application for a job or credit, etc. we do not put down "God" in the space which says "father's name?"

In Acts 7:2-53, Stephen addressed the council. He used the word "father(s)" 17 times. Stephen knew what Jesus had said about "father," and yet he used the word. Stephen knew what Jesus meant.

Jesus also tells us that we should not be called teachers. But we have all heard the terms "Sunday School Teachers," and we accept that. When we ask a child, "Who is your teacher?", we do not expect the child to reply, "I have only one teacher, the Messiah."

What does history tell us?

> From earliest times, bishops were called "father" because they ordained priests, thus they "beget fathers to the Church." (Epiphanius d. 403 A.D.). St. Jerome (d. 420 A.D.) says that bishops should be content that they are "father" and not "lord."
>
> The heads of monasteries were called "father" – the word "Abbot" coming from "Abba" which is a familiar word for "father".
>
> The title "Father" was reserved for priests of religious orders; for example, Franciscans, Dominicans, etc. Before the Protestant Revolt, the parish clergy were called "Sir." This title continued to be used by the ministers in the Protestant churches.
>
> The custom, especially in countries where English is spoken, of addressing ALL priests as "Father" seems to have been an Irish custom which was spread by Irish immigration.

Is Everything in The Bible

Some say if it is not in the Bible it is not true.

Others say that not everything is mentioned in the Bible.

What Is The Truth?

The following are **some** of the things which are not mentioned by name in the Bible, and yet many Christians believe.

1. The word "Trinity," meaning three persons in one God, each equal to the other, is not in the Bible. The word was invented by the Catholic Church to try to explain somewhat the mystery of there being Three Persons in one God, as is revealed by God. The Athanasian Creed, dating from the late 4th century, was written during the time of St. Athanasius (297-373), bishop of Alexandria, but probably not by him. It states, "the Catholic

Faith is this, that we worship One God in Trinity, and Trinity in Unity." The Council of Nicaea I (A.D. 325) said that Jesus is of one substance with God the Father. It explained the absolute unity between God and Jesus. The Council of Canstantinople (A.D. 381) said the same about the Holy Spirit as Nicaea said about Jesus. St. Augustine (345 -430) wrote *De Trinitate* (about the Trinity).

2. The word "Rapture" is not mentioned in the Bible.
3. The words "Altar Call" is not mentioned in the Bible.
4. The word "Incarnation" (meaning the Son of God took on flesh) is not mentioned in the Bible.
5. A list of inspired books which make up the Canon of Scripture (a list of the books to be included in "The Bible") is not in the Bible.
6. The Sabbath Day is Saturday. Exodus 20:8 tells us to keep the Sabbath day holy. It is not written down in the New Testament that the Apostles had the authority to change the Sabbath from Saturday to Sunday, yet all Christians observe the Sabbath on Sunday.
7. That the Bible *alone* is to be used as the sole rule of faith is not in the Bible.
8. That one is saved by faith *alone* is not in the Bible.
9. That one accepts Jesus Christ as one's personal Lord and Savior is not in the Bible.
10. That Baptism is for adults only is not mentioned in the Bible.

In John's Gospel 21:25, John says that there are many things that Jesus did and that the whole world would not be able to hold the books that would tell about them.

Early Names of the Followers of Jesus Christ

1. **Disciples**: The followers of Jesus were first called "His Disciples" in Luke 6:17.
2. **The Way**: Next, they were called "the Way" in Acts 9:2, when Paul asked for letters giving him authority to bring members of

the Way from Damascus to Jerusalem. In Acts 19:23, the followers of Jesus were called "the Way."

3. **Christians:** Then in Acts 11:26, they were called "Christians". This was in Antioch. They were also called Christians in Acts 26:28 and 1 Peter 4:16.
4. **Beloved of God**: In Romans 1:7, Paul calls them "Beloved of God".
5. **Saints**: In Ephesians 1:1, Paul calls the Ephesians holy ones or saints.
6. **The Church**: Then they were called "The Church". This is the most common name used in the New Testament for the followers of Jesus (Acts 9:31). Jesus used the name "Church" Himself when He said in Matthew 16:18 to Peter, "... you are Peter, and upon this rock I will build my church, and the gates of hell shall not prevail against it." Jesus called the Church, "My Church". He is the person Who established it. He said that His Church would never be destroyed, and that He would be with His Church always. (Matthew 28:20).
7. **Catholic**: Finally, the followers of Jesus Christ were called "Catholic". "Where the bishop is present there let the people gather, just as where Jesus Christ is, there is the Catholic Church." This was written by Ignatius of Antioch in his Letter to the Smyrnaeans around the year 107 A.D. For Ignatius, "Catholic Church" meant "the Universal Church," the Church spread all over the known world.

The Pope

Some say that Jesus appointed Peter to be head of the Apostle and that the Pope today is the Successor of Peter.

Others say that Peter was just one of the Apostles and had no authority over the others.

What Is The Truth?

In the Catholic Church there is a great amount of emphasis put upon Peter and the successors of Peter – the Popes. Is there any scriptural and historical evidence to support this practice? Yes. Let us look at the evidence from the Bible first.

1. Whenever we find a list of the Apostles, we find that Peter is always named first.
    a. Matthew 10:2 gives the names of the twelve Apostles. The first name is Simon, called Peter.
    b. Jesus appointed twelve. Simon, whom he named Peter, is named first. (Mark 3:14-19)
    c. Jesus chose Twelve, whom he also named Apostles: Simon, whom he named Peter and his brother Andrew..." (Luke 6:13-16)
    d. Acts 1:13 lists the names of His Apostles and Peter is first on the list: Peter and John and James and Andrew, Philip and Thomas, Bartholomew and Matthew, James son of Alphaeus, Simon the Zealot, and Judas son of James.
2. At times, Peter is the only one mentioned. In Luke 9:20, Jesus asked the Apostles, "Who do you say that I am?" Peter answered, "The Messiah of God." Also, see Matthew 16:15-16 and Mark 8:27-29.
3. Peter was usually the one who spoke for the Apostles.
    a. Peter asked Jesus if someone sins against him, how often does he have to forgive that person? As many as seven times? (Matthew 18:21)
    b. Peter asked Jesus if the parable was meant for them or for everyone. (Luke 12:41)
    c. Jesus asked the Twelve if they want to leave Him? Simon Peter answered Him, "Master, to whom shall we go? You have the words of eternal life. We have come to believe and are convinced that You are the Holy One of God." (John 6: 67-69)
    d. Peter walked on water. (Matthew 14:28-32)
    e. The collectors of the temple tax came to Peter and said, "Doesn't your teacher pay the temple tax?" (Matthew 17:24)

   f. Peter said to Jesus, "We have given up everything and followed you." (Mark 10:28)
4. Peter is the one who speaks to the crowd after the descent of the Holy Spirit. (Acts2:14-40)
5. Peter in the name of Jesus Christ, the Nazorean, cured the crippled man. (Acts 3:6-7)
6. Peter ordered that those who had received the gift of the Holy Spirit should be baptized. (Acts 10:46-48)

The following is a very important passage of Scripture dealing with Jesus and Peter:

> (Matthew 16:16-19) Simon Peter said to Jesus, "You are the Messiah, the Son of the living God." Jesus addressed Peter saying that he is blessed. Flesh and blood did not reveal this truth to him, but Jesus' Father in heaven. And so, Jesus said to Peter, "You are Peter, and upon this rock I will build My church, and the gates of hell shall not prevail against it. I will give to you the keys to the kingdom of heaven. Whatever you bind on earth shall be bound in heaven; and whatever you loose on earth shall be loosed in heaven."

Here, God, the Father, revealed to Peter that Jesus was the "anointed one," the Son of the Living God, and Peter expresses this.

Then Jesus changes Simon's name to Peter when he says, "You are Peter, and on this rock..." It is like saying, "You are Rock and, on this rock, I will build My Church. "Peter" means "rock." In the Aramaic language which Jesus and the church in Palestine spoke, the two words are identical, "You are KEPHA, and on this KEPHA I will build My Church." Jesus says that He will build His Church on Peter, the rock. We know this Church is to be a visible church, because Jesus says in Matthew 18:17, if anyone refuses to listen to them, tell the Church. If anyone refuses to listen even to the Church, then treat these people as you would a Gentile or a tax collector.

Jesus goes on to say that the gates of Hades shall not prevail against His Church. In other words, death would not overcome His Church. It would always continue. When Peter would die, another would take his place. Satan would not be able to take over the office of Peter because it would be protected by God. The office remains, even when the occupant changes.

The "keys of the kingdom" are a symbol of authority given only to the most trusted servant. If one had the keys it meant that when he shut, nobody could open, and when he opened, nobody could shut. If one had the keys to a city, it meant that he could let in or out whomever he wished. A similar idea is in Isaiah 22:22. "I will place the key of the House of David on his shoulder; when he opens, no one shall shut, when he shuts, no one shall open."

Jesus gave Peter the power to "bind" and "loose." That means that Peter has the power to make the rules for the visible church on earth. Of course, he cannot change the rules given by God, but he can make the rules in support of what God has revealed; for example, how long we are to fast before we receive Holy Communion.

Jesus also gave the power to bind and loose to the apostles. However, it was only Peter who got the "keys" – the symbol of supreme authority. And that is why the successor of Peter today, the Pope, has the supreme authority in the Church. We have other examples from Scripture pointing out the special position of Peter:

> Simon, Simon, behold Satan has demanded to sift all of you like wheat, but I have prayed that your own faith may not fail; and once you have turned back, you must strengthen your brothers. (Luke 22:31-32)

Jesus prayed that Peter's faith would never fail, and that he would be a guide to the others. Here we see the role of leadership that Peter and his successors, the popes, would have in relationship to the other Apostles and their successors, the bishops.

Turning to John's Gospel 21:15-17, we find Jesus asking Peter 3 times, "Do you love me? Peter answered 3 times that he does love Jesus. Peter proclaimed three times that he loved Jesus in order to make up for the three times he denied Jesus. Then Jesus, who is the Good Shepherd, gave Peter full authority when He said, "Feed My Sheep."

What does history tell us about Peter and his successors as the visible head of the Church on earth?

There is overwhelming historical evidence that Peter went to Rome, and was Bishop of Rome. He was martyred there in 64 or 67 A.D. and was succeeded as bishop of Rome by Linus, who had been ordained by Peter. The Apostle John was still alive in Ephesus (in modern day Turkey). John would have been the logical successor to Peter as head of the Church, but he never claimed that position. About ten years later, Anacletus (Cletus) succeeded Linus. Clement I followed him around 90 A.D. John the Apostle was still alive, but still did not put himself as head of the Church.

In 96 A.D., Clement I, Bishop of Rome, wrote a letter to the Christian Church in Corinth. This is the first Christian document that we have outside of the New Testament. It was preserved for centuries with great care and was frequently read. The letter is of tremendous importance because it shows that the successors of St. Peter as Bishop of Rome had authority over the whole Church. The letter was written to settle disputes which had arisen among the Christians in Corinth.

Clement knew Peter personally and mentioned his martyrdom in Rome as a fact to all Christians. He then writes about the apostolic succession: "The Apostles preached the gospel to us from the Lord Jesus Christ. Christ, therefore, is from God, and the Apostles are from Christ... as they (the Apostles) preached, therefore, in the countryside and in the cities, they appointed their first fruits – and having tested them through the Spirit – to be bishops and deacons of the future believers."

He goes on to warn the Corinthians about the dangers of friction among themselves and then ends his warning with his very important sentence. "If some shall disobey the words which have been spoken by Him (Christ) through us (Clement) let them know that they will involve themselves in no small transgression and danger."

This is a clear statement that the Bishop of Rome has the authority from God over the Church at Corinth, and to disobey him in a

Church matter would be a serious sin, even though they had a local bishop.

Also, the fact that the Corinthians preserved this letter and read it frequently on Sundays, shows that they accepted Clement's authority over them. Something else can be pointed out also. The language in Corinth was Greek. Rome was Latin-speaking. Normally, no one from the West would have authority in the East – but Clement's authority was accepted. It was accepted because he was the successor of Peter and head of the whole Church. All this happened before the death of many who knew Peter in Rome. They knew what Peter taught and how he was accepted by the Christians as holding the keys to the kingdom of heaven which Jesus Christ had given to him. They accepted Peter as the chief of the Apostles, and they accepted the Bishop of Rome as successor of Peter and Chief Bishop.

Have You Been Saved?

Some people say that if at one point in their lives they "accept Christ as their personal Savior," then they will get to heaven. They may lead good lives after this acceptance, but they think that living a good life is not necessary. Their salvation is certain. It cannot be undone. They just "know" for sure that they have been saved now that they have accepted Jesus Christ.

Other people say that there is a lot more involved in getting to heaven than accepting Jesus.

What Is The Truth?

What does the Bible say?

Paul said that we should work out their salvation with fear and trembling. (Philippians 2:12)

Paul told the Corinthians that he drives his body and trains it, for fear that, after having preached to others, he, himself, should be disqualified. (1 Corinthians 9:27)

Paul says in Romans 5:2 that we boast in hope of sharing the glory of God. And in 1 Cor 10:12, Paul says that a person who thinks he is standing secure should take care not to fall.

Peter writes to people who have accepted Jesus Christ then go back to worldly ways again: He says their last condition is worse than the first. (2 Peter 2:20-21)

Paul talks about the kindness and severity of God. God is severe toward those who fell, but kind to those who remain in His kindness. (Romans 11:22)

If the people to whom they were writing were already saved, then Peter would not have written that it would have been better for some not to have known the way of righteousness than to have turned away from it. In other words, Peter did not accept the idea of being saved just by accepting Jesus as one's personal Savior and that was all that was needed. Paul wrote the same idea to the Romans.

In 1 Corinthians 4:3-5, Paul tells the Corinthians that they should judge nothing before the time, but that the Lord will praise each one when He comes. Paul says that we cannot judge ourselves as saved - the Lord is the One who does that.

<u>So, who will be saved?</u>

Jesus gives the answer in Matthew 7:21: None of those who says to Him, "Lord, Lord," will enter the kingdom of heaven, but only the one who does the Will of His Father in heaven.

In Romans 2:6, Paul says that God will repay everyone according to his works.

In 2 Corinthians 5:10, Paul says that we must all appear for judgment before Christ. Then each one may receive recompense, according to what he did in the body, whether good or evil.

In Matthew 10:22, Jesus says that whoever endures to the end will be saved. He says the same in Mark 13:13 and Matthew 24:13.

So, in order to be saved one must keep working at it. It is not a one-shot deal. In Matthew 25, Jesus advises everyone to be always ready for His coming.

The Catholic Church teaches that a person is saved if there is no mortal sin on their soul at the time of their death. The Church takes into account:

1. What the Word of God says, and
2. The fact that God has given us the gift of Free Will by which we can choose good or evil at any time during our life – we are free, we are never locked into being "saved" or "unsaved" – we work out our salvation with fear and trembling (Philippians 2:12), and hope we will endure to the end (Matthew 10:22).

So, when we are asked "Have you been saved?" What do we say?

We can say...

"I have been saved,"
"I am being saved,"
"I hope to be saved."

To explain further:

1. "I have been saved. I was saved at 3:00 P.M. on Good Friday in 33 A.D." It is a fact that Jesus Christ died on the cross and rose from the dead in order for us to get to heaven. Jesus Christ has redeemed the world and has done his part to save the world.
2. "I am being saved." We are still, like Paul (1 Corinthians 9:24-27) running the race to achieve our salvation. Jesus is working in our life.
3. "I hope to be saved." We must keep working at our faith in God, our love of God, and doing the Will of God until we die. We hope that God will give us the grace to choose whatever will help us on the road to heaven. In this way, "I hope to be saved."

The teaching of the Catholic Church and the teaching of the Bible are the same. And that teaching is that we strive always to do the Will of Our Father, God, and that we never give up but keep striving to get to heaven. The test is not over until we have drawn our last breath.

> You will know the Truth, and the Truth will set you free.
> Jn 8:32

Should Catholics Believe in The Rapture?

The idea of the Rapture is based on 1 Thessalonians 4:16-17. Some imagine Jesus coming secretly and snatching certain people out of their cars, places of work, houses and even airplanes in order to meet the Lord in the air. It is not known when this will happen. This idea of a secret rapture or being secretly transported to another place of ecstatic joy or delight, has become very popular in recent years. The idea became popular because of the books by Evangelicals, Tim LaHaye and Jerry Jenkins. These are the *Left Behind* books which were also made into the *Left Behind* movies.

These have captured people's imagination. La Haye and Jenkins believe that Jesus will secretly and invisibly snatch true believers, living and dead, up into heaven. This will cause confusion all over the world. Then the devil will take control of the world through the antichrist. A great tribulation will take place. After that is over, Jesus will come back so that everyone can see Him. He will defeat the forces of evil and that will be the end of history.

Catholics believe that Paul was talking in a general way about the Second and Final coming of Jesus and the resurrection from the dead (Catechism of the Catholic Church 997-1001).

What Is The Truth?

This is a new idea which has been around for only about 150 years. There is nothing in the Bible to support this idea of a secret coming of Jesus. The Bible tells us the Parousia, or Second Coming of Christ, will be known to the whole world (Matthew 24-27, 30-31, Mark 14:62, 1 Thessalonians 4:14-17, 2 Thessalonians 1:7-8, 1 Corinthians 15:51-52, Revelation 1:7).

The Lord will return on clouds of glory. Angels and saints will be with Him. There will be a trumpet blast to proclaim their coming. The faithful on earth will be gathered to Him. The remainder of the world will be terrified.

Catholics focus on the condition of the individual soul at the time of death and not on speculation about how and when Jesus will return.

The concept of the "rapture" is based on a misinterpretation of 1 Thessalonians 4:16-17:

> *For the Lord himself shall descend from heaven with a shout, with the voice of the archangel, and with the trumpet of God: and the dead in Christ shall rise first: Then we which are alive and remain shall be caught up together with them in the clouds, to meet the Lord in the air: and so, shall we ever be with the Lord* (KJV)

To understand 1 Thessalonians 4:16-17, we must look to the background of why St. Paul is writing this letter. One of the questions which had not been answered was whether the dead would be at any disadvantage in respect to the living when the Parousia of the Lord came. St. Paul's answer is in these verses in 1 Thessalonians, and it is to the effect that no one will have an advantage; when the Parousia comes, the living and the dead will meet Jesus together in their glorified bodies ("in the air" – since they and their bodies have been changed from being corruptible to being incorruptible and they have become immortal rather than mortal).

Rather than concern ourselves about the timing of such things as the "rapture" or the Parousia, we should read the verses in 1 Thessalonians which follow the ones just quoted:

> *Therefore encourage each other with these words. Now, brothers and sisters, about times and dates we do not need to write to you, for you know very well that the day of the Lord will come like a thief in the night. While people are saying, "Peace and safety," destruction will come on them suddenly, as labor pains on a pregnant woman, and they will not escape.* (1 Thessalonians 4:18-5:3, NIV)

We must concern ourselves with living as if every day and hour may be our last on earth; so that we may be prepared to meet the divine Judge and be deemed worthy of enjoying eternity with Him.

Your word is truth. Jn17:17

I speak the truth. Jn 8:45

The World's Greatest Robbery

The Truth Has Been Stolen from Millions Over the Last 500 Years

	Teachings of THE CATHOLIC CHURCH AT THE TIME OF THE APOSTLES	Teachings of CATHOLIC CHURCH TODAY	Teachings of PROTESTANT CHURCHES TODAY
BAPTISM	**Jn 3:5** Jesus said a person must be born again of water & the Holy Spirit to get to heaven. **Mt 28:19-20** Jesus told the Apostles to go teach & baptize. **Acts 2:38** Peter said that people must reform & be baptized. **Titus 3:5** Paul said that Christ saved us through baptism.	Same Truth as Jesus and the Apostles Taught	Some churches have Baptism. This Truth is Stolen from others.
CONFESSION	**Jn 20:19-23** Jesus gave the power to forgive sins to Apostles. **2 Cor 5:18** Paul said that God, through Christ, gave the Apostles the ministry of reconciliation.	Same Truth as Jesus and the Apostles Taught	This Truth is Stolen from the people.
EUCHARIST	**Lk 22:19-20** Jesus changed bread & wine into His Body & Blood. **1 Cor 10:16** Paul said the cup & bread are a sharing in the Blood & Body of Christ. **Jn 6:54** Jesus said we must eat His Flesh & drink His Blood	Same Truth as Jesus and the Apostles Taught	This Truth is Stolen from the people.

	Teachings of THE CATHOLIC CHURCH AT THE TIME OF THE APOSTLES	**Teachings of CATHOLIC CHURCH TODAY**	**Teachings of PROTESTANT CHURCHES TODAY**
CONFIRMATION	**Acts 8:15-17** Peter & John laid hands on the people in Samaria & they received the Holy Spirit. **Acts 19:6** Paul laid his hands on the people in Ephesus & the Holy Spirit came on them.	Same Truth as Jesus and the Apostles Taught	This Truth is Stolen from the people.
MATRIMONY	**Gen 2:24** God instituted marriage when He created Adam & Eve. **Mk 10:11-12** & **Mt 19:3-9** Jesus said if one divorces and marries another, he/she commits adultery. **Jn 2:1-11** Jesus preformed His first miracle at the Wedding at Cana, thus instituting the Sacrament of Matrimony.	Same Truth as Jesus and the Apostles Taught	Allows Divorce & Remarriage – This Truth is Stolen from the people.
HOLY ORDERS (PRIESTHOOD)	**Lk 22:19-20** After Jesus changed bread & wine into His Body & Blood at the Last Supper, He told His Apostles to do what He just did; that is, to offer sacrifice, thus instituting **the** Priesthood. **Jn 20:21-23** Jesus gave His Apostles the power to forgive sins.	Same Truth as Jesus and the Apostles Taught	This Truth is Stolen from the people.

	Teachings of THE CATHOLIC CHURCH AT THE TIME OF THE APOSTLES	Teachings of CATHOLIC CHURCH TODAY	Teachings of PROTESTANT CHURCHES TODAY
ANOINTING OF THE SICK	**Mk 6:13** Jesus sent His Apostles to anoint the sick with oil. **Jam 5:14** James said the priests should come to pray with & anoint the sick.	Same Truth as Jesus and the Apostles Taught	This Truth is Stolen from the people.
PRAYING FOR THE DEAD	**Rev 21:27** John said nothing defiled shall enter heaven. **2 Mac 12:38-46** Judas Maccabeus had sacrifice offered for the dead. **Mt 12:32** Jesus says that some sins are not forgiven in the next world.	Same Truth as Jesus and the Apostles Taught	This Truth is Stolen from the people.
JESUS FOUNDED A CHURCH	**Mt 16:16** JESUS CHRIST: Jesus said, "I will build MY Church …"	Same Truth as Jesus and the Apostles Taught	Human beings set up churches & creeds independent of Jesus & His teachings. This Truth is Stolen from the people.
JESUS APPOINTED PETER HEAD OF THE CHURCH	**Mt 16:17-19** Jesus told Peter He would give to him the keys to the kingdom of heaven. **Jn 21:15-17** Jesus told Peter to "Feed My sheep."; that is, the whole flock.	Same Truth as Jesus and the Apostles Taught	This Truth is Stolen from the people.

	Teachings of THE CATHOLIC CHURCH AT THE TIME OF THE APOSTLES	Teachings of CATHOLIC CHURCH TODAY	Teachings of PROTESTANT CHURCHES TODAY
INFALLIBLE TEACHING AUTHORITY GIVEN TO THE CHURCH	**Jn 18:37** Jesus said He came into the world to bear witness to the Truth. **1Thes 2:13** Paul said the message He gave was not the word of men, but God. **Acts 15:28** The Apostles told the people in Antioch that the decision made was the decision of the Holy Spirit & theirs. **Gal 1:8** Paul said a curse should fall on anyone, man or angel, who preaches a Gospel different to the Gospel He preached. **1 Tim 3:15** The Church of the living God, the pillar and ground of truth.	Same Truth as Jesus and the Apostles Taught	This Truth is Stolen from the people.
BIBLE	Wrote the New Testament and preserved the Old and New Testament.	Decided what books are inspired in the Old & New Testaments, thus giving us the Bible	Stole Seven Books from the Old Testament. This Truth is Stolen from the people.
INTERPRETATION OF SCRIPTURE	**2 Pet 1:20** Peter said there is no personal interpretation of Scripture.	Same Truth as Jesus and the Apostles Taught	Each person can interpret the Bible as he/she sees fit. This Truth is Stolen from the people.

	Teachings of THE CATHOLIC CHURCH AT THE TIME OF THE APOSTLES	**Teachings of CATHOLIC CHURCH TODAY**	**Teachings of PROTESTANT CHURCHES TODAY**
UNITY	**Jn 17:11** Jesus prayed that His followers would be one as the Father and He are One. **Eph 4:4-5** Paul said there is only One Body, One Spirit, One Lord, One Faith, One Baptism, One God & Father of all.	Same Truth as Jesus and the Apostles Taught	This Truth of Oneness was stolen from the people resulting in over 34,000 churches with different beliefs instead of one Church with one set of beliefs.
NEVER ENDING STRIVING TO GET TO HEAVEN	**Phil 2:12** Paul tells us to work out our salvation in fear & trembling. **Mk 13:13, Mt 24:13** Jesus tells us that we must persevere to be saved.	Same Truth as Jesus and the Apostles Taught	This Truth is Stolen from the people.
MARY IS HONORED	**Lk 1:28-35** The angel Gabriel told Mary that God favored her. **Ex 20:12** Jesus obeyed the 4th Commandment & thus, honored His mother. **Lk 1:35** The Holy Spirit came upon her.	Same Truth as Jesus and the Apostles Taught	This Truth is Stolen from the people.

	Teachings of THE CATHOLIC CHURCH AT THE TIME OF THE APOSTLES	**Teachings of CATHOLIC CHURCH TODAY**	**Teachings of PROTESTANT CHURCHES TODAY**
BAPTISM OF INFANTS	**Col 2:11-12** Paul says Baptism replaced circumcision. Usually, only infants were circumcised under the Old Law. **Acts 16:15** Lydia & her whole household were baptized. Whole households would include children. **Acts 16:33** A Philippian jailer & all his family were baptized. **1 Cor 1:16** Paul baptized Stephanas' household._	Same Truth as Jesus and the Apostles Taught	The Truth is Stolen from the people.

The List of Popes

1. St. Peter (32-67)
2. St. Linus (67-76)
3. St. Anacletus (Cletus) (76-88)
4. St. Clement I (88-97)
5. St. Evaristus (97-105)
6. St. Alexander I (105-115)
7. St. Sixtus I (115-125) Also called Xystus I
8. St. Telesphorus (125-136)
9. St. Hyginus (136-140)
10. St. Pius I (140-155)
11. St. Anicetus (155-166)
12. St. Soter (166-175)
13. St. Eleutherius (175-189)
14. St. Victor I (189-199)
15. St. Zephyrinus (199-217)
16. St. Callistus I (217-22) Callistus and the following three popes were opposed by St. Hippolytus, antipope (217-236)
17. St. Urban I (222-30)
18. St. Pontian (230-35)
19. St. Anterus (235-36)
20. St. Fabian (236-50)
21. St. Cornelius (251-53) Opposed by Novatian, antipope (251)
22. St. Lucius I (253-54)
23. St. Stephen I (254-257)
24. St. Sixtus II (257-258)
25. St. Dionysius (260-268)
26. St. Felix I (269-274)
27. St. Eutychian (275-283)
28. St. Caius (283-296) Also called Gaius
29. St. Marcellinus (296-304)
30. St. Marcellus I (308-309)
31. St. Eusebius (309 or 310)
32. St. Miltiades (311-14)
33. St. Sylvester I (314-35)
34. St. Marcus (336)
35. St. Julius I (337-52)
36. Liberius (352-66) Opposed by Felix II, antipope (355-365)
37. St. Damasus I (366-84) Opposed by Ursicinus, antipope (366-367)
38. St. Siricius (384-99)
39. St. Anastasius I (399-401)
40. St. Innocent I (401-17)
41. St. Zosimus (417-18)
42. St. Boniface I (418-22) Opposed by Eulalius, antipope (418-419)
43. St. Celestine I (422-32)
44. St. Sixtus III (432-40)
45. St. Leo I (the Great) (440-61)
46. St. Hilarius (461-68)

47. St. Simplicius (468-83)
48. St. Felix III (II) (483-92)
49. St. Gelasius I (492-96)
50. Anastasius II (496-98)
51. St. Symmachus (498-514) Opposed by Laurentius, antipope (498-501)
52. St. Hormisdas (514-23)
53. St. John I (523-26)
54. St. Felix IV (III) (526-30)
55. Boniface II (530-32) Opposed by Dioscorus, antipope (530)
56. John II (533-35)
57. St. Agapetus I (535-36) Also called Agapitus I
58. St. Silverius (536-37)
59. Vigilius (537-55)
60. Pelagius I (556-61)
61. John III (561-74)
62. Benedict I (575-79)
63. Pelagius II (579-90)
64. St. Gregory I (the Great) (590-604)
65. Sabinian (604-606)
66. Boniface III (607)
67. St. Boniface IV (608-15)
68. St. Deusdedit (Adeodatus I) (615-18)
69. Boniface V (619-25)
70. Honorius I (625-38)
71. Severinus (640)
72. John IV (640-42)
73. Theodore I (642-49)
74. St. Martin I (649-55)
75. St. Eugene I (655-57)
76. St. Vitalian (657-72)
77. Adeodatus (II) (672-76)
78. Donus (676-78)
79. St. Agatho (678-81)
80. St. Leo II (682-83)
81. St. Benedict II (684-85)
82. John V (685-86)
83. Conon (686-87)
84. St. Sergius I (687-701) Opposed by Theodore and Paschal, antipopes (687)
85. John VI (701-05)
86. John VII (705-07)
87. Sisinnius (708)
88. Constantine (708-15)
89. St. Gregory II (715-31)
90. St. Gregory III (731-41)
91. St. Zachary (741-52) Stephen II followed Zachary, but because he died before being consecrated, modern lists omit him
92. Stephen II (III) (752-57)
93. St. Paul I (757-67)
94. Stephen III (IV) (767-72) Opposed by Constantine II (767) and Philip (768), antipopes (767)
95. Adrian I (772-95)
96. St. Leo III (795-816)
97. Stephen IV (V) (816-17)
98. St. Paschal I (817-24)
99. Eugene II (824-27)

100. Valentine (827)
101. Gregory IV (827-44)
102. Sergius II (844-47) Opposed by John, antipope
103. St. Leo IV (847-55)
104. Benedict III (855-58) Opposed by Anastasius, antipope (855)
105. St. Nicholas I (the Great) (858-67)
106. Adrian II (867-72)
107. John VIII (872-82)
108. Marinus I (882-84)
109. St. Adrian III (884-85)
110. Stephen V (VI) (885-91)
111. Formosus (891-96)
112. Boniface VI (896)
113. Stephen VI (VII) (896-97)
114. Romanus (897)
115. Theodore II (897)
116. John IX (898-900)
117. Benedict IV (900-03)
118. Leo V (903) Opposed by Christopher, antipope (903-904)
119. Sergius III (904-11)
120. Anastasius III (911-13)
121. Lando (913-14)
122. John X (914-28)
123. Leo VI (928)
124. Stephen VIII (929-31)
125. John XI (931-35)
126. Leo VII (936-39)
127. Stephen IX (939-42)
128. Marinus II (942-46)
129. Agapetus II (946-55)
130. John XII (955-63)
131. Leo VIII (963-64)
132. Benedict V (964)
133. John XIII (965-72)
134. Benedict VI (973-74)
135. Benedict VII (974-83) Benedict and John XIV were opposed by Boniface VII, antipope (974; 984-985)
136. John XIV (983-84)
137. John XV (985-96)
138. Gregory V (996-99) Opposed by John XVI, antipope (997-998)
139. Sylvester II (999-1003)
140. John XVII (1003)
141. John XVIII (1003-09)
142. Sergius IV (1009-12)
143. Benedict VIII (1012-24) Opposed by Gregory, antipope (1012)
144. John XIX (1024-32)
145. Benedict IX (1032-45) He appears on this list three separate times, because he was twice deposed and restored
146. Sylvester III (1045) Considered by some to be an antipope
147. Benedict IX (1045)
148. Gregory VI (1045-46)
149. Clement II (1046-47)
150. Benedict IX (1047-48)
151. Damasus II (1048)

152. St. Leo IX (1049-54)
153. Victor II (1055-57)
154. Stephen X (1057-58)
155. Nicholas II (1058-61) Opposed by Benedict X, antipope (1058)
156. Alexander II (1061-73) Opposed by Honorius II, antipope (1061-1072)
157. St. Gregory VII (1073-85) Gregory and the following three popes were opposed by Guibert ("Clement III"), antipope (1080-1100)
158. Blessed Victor III (1086-87)
159. Blessed Urban II (1088-99)
160. Paschal II (1099-1118) Opposed by Theodoric (1100), Aleric (1102) and Maginulf ("Sylvester IV", 1105-1111), antipopes (1100)
161. Gelasius II (1118-19) Opposed by Burdin ("Gregory VIII"), antipope (1118)
162. Callistus II (1119-24)
163. Honorius II (1124-30) Opposed by Celestine II, antipope (1124)
164. Innocent II (1130-43) Opposed by Anacletus II (1130-1138) and Gregory Conti ("Victor IV") (1138), antipopes (1138)
165. Celestine II (1143-44)
166. Lucius II (1144-45)
167. Blessed Eugene III (1145-53)
168. Anastasius IV (1153-54)
169. Adrian IV (1154-59)
170. Alexander III (1159-81) Opposed by Octavius ("Victor IV") (1159-1164), Pascal III (1165-1168), Callistus III (1168-1177) and Innocent III (1178-1180), antipopes
171. Lucius III (1181-85)
172. Urban III (1185-87)
173. Gregory VIII (1187)
174. Clement III (1187-91)
175. Celestine III (1191-98)
176. Innocent III (1198-1216)
177. Honorius III (1216-27)
178. Gregory IX (1227-41)
179. Celestine IV (1241)
180. Innocent IV (1243-54)
181. Alexander IV (1254-61)
182. Urban IV (1261-64)
183. Clement IV (1265-68)
184. Blessed Gregory X (1271-76)
185. Blessed Innocent V (1276)
186. Adrian V (1276)
187. John XXI (1276-77)
188. Nicholas III (1277-80)
189. Martin IV (1281-85)
190. Honorius IV (1285-87)
191. Nicholas IV (1288-92)
192. St. Celestine V (1294)
193. Boniface VIII (1294-1303)

194. Blessed Benedict XI (1303-04)
195. Clement V (1305-14)
196. John XXII (1316-34) Opposed by Nicholas V, antipope (1328-1330)
197. Benedict XII (1334-42)
198. Clement VI (1342-52)
199. Innocent VI (1352-62)
200. Blessed Urban V (1362-70)
201. Gregory XI (1370-78)
202. Urban VI (1378-89) Opposed by Robert of Geneva ("Clement VII"), antipope (1378-1394)
203. Boniface IX (1389-1404) Opposed by Robert of Geneva ("Clement VII") (1378-1394), Pedro de Luna ("Benedict XIII") (1394-1417) and Baldassare Cossa ("John XXIII") (1400-1415), antipopes
204. Innocent VII (1404-06) Opposed by Pedro de Luna ("Benedict XIII") (1394-1417) and Baldassare Cossa ("John XXIII") (1400-1415), antipopes
205. Gregory XII (1406-15) Opposed by Pedro de Luna ("Benedict XIII") (1394-1417), Baldassare Cossa ("John XXIII") (1400-1415), and Pietro Philarghi ("Alexander V") (1409-1410), antipopes
206. Martin V (1417-31)
207. Eugene IV (1431-47) Opposed by Amadeus of Savoy ("Felix V"), antipope (1439-1449)
208. Nicholas V (1447-55)
209. Callistus III (1455-58)
210. Pius II (1458-64)
211. Paul II (1464-71)
212. Sixtus IV (1471-84)
213. Innocent VIII (1484-92)
214. Alexander VI (1492-1503)
215. Pius III (1503)
216. Julius II (1503-13)
217. Leo X (1513-21)
218. Adrian VI (1522-23)
219. Clement VII (1523-34)
220. Paul III (1534-49)
221. Julius III (1550-55)
222. Marcellus II (1555)
223. Paul IV (1555-59)
224. Pius IV (1559-65)
225. St. Pius V (1566-72)
226. Gregory XIII (1572-85)
227. Sixtus V (1585-90)
228. Urban VII (1590)
229. Gregory XIV (1590-91)
230. Innocent IX (1591)
231. Clement VIII (1592-1605)
232. Leo XI (1605)

233. Paul V (1605-21)
234. Gregory XV (1621-23)
235. Urban VIII (1623-44)
236. Innocent X (1644-55)
237. Alexander VII (1655-67)
238. Clement IX (1667-69)
239. Clement X (1670-76)
240. Blessed Innocent XI (1676-89)
241. Alexander VIII (1689-91)
242. Innocent XII (1691-1700)
243. Clement XI (1700-21)
244. Innocent XIII (1721-24)
245. Benedict XIII (1724-30)
246. Clement XII (1730-40)
247. Benedict XIV (1740-58)
248. Clement XIII (1758-69)
249. Clement XIV (1769-74)
250. Pius VI (1775-99)
251. Pius VII (1800-23)
252. Leo XII (1823-29)
253. Pius VIII (1829-30)
254. Gregory XVI (1831-46)
255. Blessed Pius IX (1846-78)
256. Leo XIII (1878-1903)
257. St. Pius X (1903-14)
258. Benedict XV (1914-22) Biographies of Benedict XV and his successors will be added at a later date
259. Pius XI (1922-39)
260. Pius XII (1939-58)
261. St. John XXIII (1958-63)
262. Paul VI (1963-78)
263. John Paul I (1978)
264. St. John Paul II (1978-2005)
265. Benedict XVI (2005-2013)
266. Francis (2013—)

Resources

THE LIST OF POPES:

APA citation. The List of Popes. (1911). In The Catholic Encyclopedia. New York: Robert Appleton Company. Retrieved March 10, 2021 from New Advent: http://www.newadvent.org/cathen/12272b.htm

MLA citation. "The List of Popes." The Catholic Encyclopedia. Vol. 12. New York: Robert Appleton Company, 1911. 10 Mar. 2021 <http://www.newadvent.org/cathen/12272b.htm>.

Ecclesiastical approbation. *Nihil Obstat.* June 1, 1911. Remy Lafort, S.T.D., Censor. *Imprimatur.* +John Cardinal Farley, Archbishop of New York.

OTHER RESOURCES USED TO CHECK INFORMATION:

Information was gathered over the years of Fr. John's priesthood. There is no way to know all of the sources used.

Information in this edition was verified using:

Britannica Books and https://www.britannica.com/
New Advent https://www.newadvent.org/
Catholic Answers https://www.catholic.com/
Encyclopedia.com https://www.encyclopedia.com/
Catholic Bible Dictionary, Scott Hahn, Double Day
Fr. Smith Instructs Jackson, Bishop Noll, Our Sunday Visitor
Faith of Millions, John A. O'Brien, 1974, Our Sunday Visitor, Inc., 200 Noll Plaza, Huntington, IN 46750
The Encyclopedia of Catholic History, Matthew Bunson, Our Sunday Visitor, Inc., 200 Noll Plaza, Huntington, IN 46750
The Modern Catholic Encyclopedia, edited by Michael Glazier and Monika Hellwig, Liturgical Press, 2950 St. John's Road, Collegeville, MN 59321

Finding Christ's Church: with a map to show the way, John A. O'Brian, 1950, Ava Maria Press.
The Origin of the Bible: Human Intervention or Divine Intervention, Dr. Brant Pitre, https://catholicproductions.com/products/the-origin-of-the-bible-human-invention-or-divine-intervention

ACKNOWLEDGMENTS

Charts were compiled by Fr. John Noone.
Drawing on Cover by Richard Marchand.
Cover design by Booknook.biz
Formatted for eBook and POD book by Booknook.biz.
Chart of History of the Catholic Church Drawn by Richard Marchand using as model a drawing by Anthony Sorado of Life Magazine
Editing and revisions by Carolyn Seal, OFS.

About the Author

John Noone was born in Ireland in December 1941. He grew up in Ireland with his family.

He was ordained on June 10, 1967 at St. Patrick's College, Carlow, Ireland and came to United States shortly after.

He received Master's Degree in Social Work from Tulane University in New Orleans in 1971 and became a citizen of the United States in 1972.

He received the following appointments: 1967- 1970 Assistant Pastor of Our Lady of the Gulf, Bay St. Louis, MS; 1970 Assistant Director of Catholic Charities; 1977 Director of Catholic Social Services for the newly established Diocese of Biloxi, MS; 1983 Pastor of three parishes – Holy Trinity in Columbia, MS, St. Paul in Tylertown, MS and St. Mary's Church, Sylvest, Ms; 1990 Pastor of St. Charles Borromeo in Picayune, MS; 2002 Pastor of Annunciation Church in Kiln, MS; 2014 Retired.

He continues working on his calling to get the truth out to all who are looking for it.

Fr. John Noone has compiled information for several CDs and books through the years of his priesthood from various sources and from his parishioners.

Made in the USA
Columbia, SC
24 July 2021

42189529R00076